SCHOLASTIC

National Curriculum
ENGLISH
TEXTBOOK

Year 6

Key Stage 2

NATIONAL CURRICULUM TEXTBOOKS

National Curriculum ENGLISH TEXTBOOK

Scholastic Education, an imprint of Scholastic Ltd
Book End, Range Road, Witney, Oxfordshire, OX29 0YD
Registered office: Westfield Road, Southam, Warwickshire CV47 0RA
www.scholastic.co.uk

© 2016, Scholastic Ltd

23456789 6789012345

British Library Cataloguing-in-Publication Data
A catalogue record for this book is available from the British Library.

ISBN 978-1407-16016-0
Printed and bound by Ashford Colour Press

All rights reserved. This book is sold subject to the condition that it shall not, by way of trade or otherwise, be lent, hired out or otherwise circulated without the publisher's prior consent in any form of binding or cover other than that in which it is published and without a similar condition, including this condition, being imposed upon the subsequent purchaser.

No part of this publication may be reproduced, stored in a retrieval system, or transmitted, in any form or by any means, electronic, mechanical, photocopying, recording or otherwise, other than for the purposes described in the content of this product, without the prior permission of the publisher. This product remains in copyright.

Every effort has been made to trace copyright holders for the works reproduced in this book, and the publishers apologise for any inadvertent omissions.

Author
Lesley and Graham Fletcher

Editorial
Rachel Morgan, Jenny Wilcox, Louise Titley, Niamh O'Carroll and Jane Jackson

Series Design
Scholastic Design Team: Nicolle Thomas and Neil Salt

Design
Oxford Designers & Illustrators Ltd

Cover Design
Scholastic Design Team: Nicolle Thomas and Neil Salt

Cover Illustration
Shutterstock / © VIGE.CO

Illustration
Judy Brown

Contents

How to use this book 5

Grammatical words

Using expanded noun phrases 6
Verbs: present perfect and past perfect tense 8
Relative clauses 9
Modal verbs 10
Adverbs of possibility 11
Subjects and objects 12
Active and passive verbs 14
The subjunctive 16

Punctuation

Commas to clarify meaning 18
Question tags 19
Hyphens 20
Bullet points 21
Colons and semi-colons in lists 22
Separating independent clauses 24
Parenthesis 26

Vocabulary

Suffixes: 'ant' or 'ent'; 'ance' or 'ence'; 'ancy' or 'ency'? 28
Prefixes: 're', 'dis' or 'mis'? 30
Adding suffixes to words ending 'fer' 31
Synonyms 32
Antonyms 33
Informal and formal vocabulary 34

Spelling

Letter strings: 'ought' 36
Letter strings: 'ough' 37
Silent letters 38
'c' or 's'? 39
Adding 'cious' or 'tious' 40
Adding 'tial' or 'cial' 41
Adding 'able' or 'ably' 42
Adding 'ible' or 'ibly' 43
'ei' after 'c' 44
Tricky words 45
Homophones 46
Using dictionaries 48
Using a theasaurus 50

Contents

Reading

Identifying main ideas	52
Identifying key details	53
Summarising main ideas	54
Retrieving and recording information	56
Making comparisons	58
Themes and conventions	60
Fact and opinion	62
Explaining and justifying inferences	64
Predicting what might happen	66
Words in context	68
Exploring words in context	69
How writers use language	70
Enhancing meaning: figurative language	72
Features of text	74
Text features contributing to meaning	75
Asking questions	76

Writing

Planning writing	78
Structuring writing	80
Building cohesion	82
Ellipsis	84
Getting verbs right	85
Précising longer pieces of writing	86
Choosing the right vocabulary and grammar	87
Describing settings and atmosphere	88
Describing characters and using dialogue	90
Editing text	92
Proofreading	94
Word list	96

How to use this book

Introduction

This book provides information and varied examples, activities and questions in a clear and consistent format, covering the National Curriculum for English for this age group.

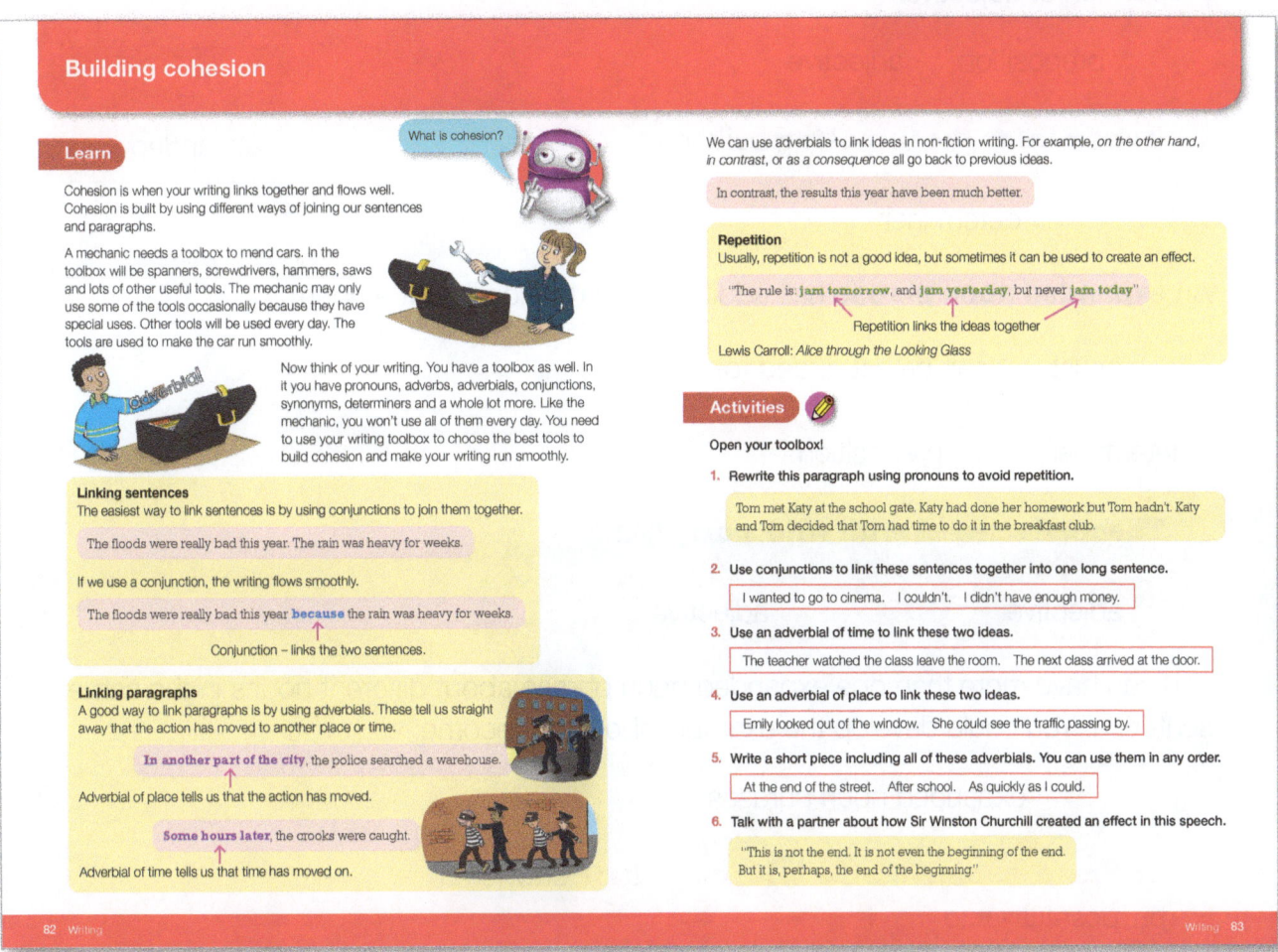

I give tips to help you!

Structure

- **Learn** – examples and explanations of the area in focus.
- **Tip** – short and simple advice to aid understanding.
- **Activities** – a focused range of questions to practice skills learned.
- **Key words** – important vocabulary to know.

Using expanded noun phrases

How do you use expanded noun phrases to give complicated information?

Learn

A noun is a word for a person, place or thing.
There are different types of noun: common (car, dog) and proper (London, Kate).

A proper noun always starts with a capital letter.

A noun phrase contains a noun as its main word and often contains a determiner, preposition or adjective.

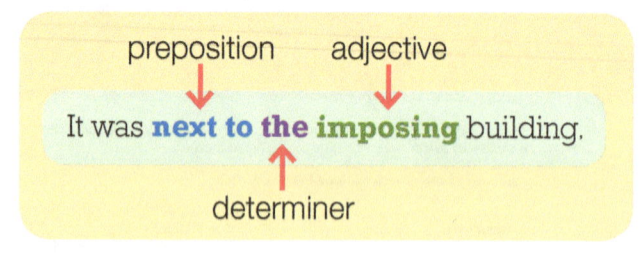

> preposition   adjective
> It was **next to the** **imposing** building.
> determiner

Key words

expanded noun phrase

An **expanded noun phrase** has additional information about a noun.

scientist   can be expanded to.

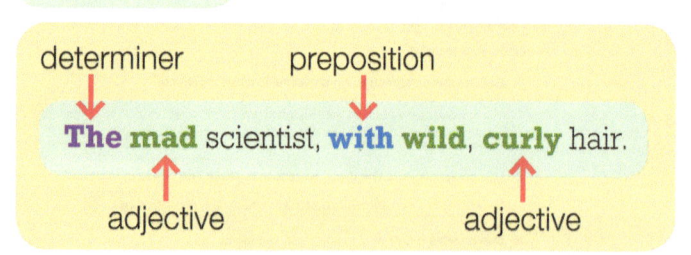

> determiner   preposition
> **The** mad scientist, **with** wild, curly hair.
> adjective   adjective

You can have more than one expanded noun phrase about different nouns in the same sentence. You could develop the example above to become:

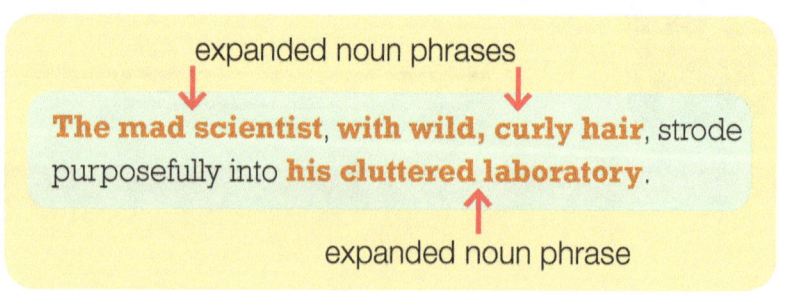

> expanded noun phrases
> **The mad scientist**, **with wild, curly hair**, strode purposefully into **his cluttered laboratory**.
> expanded noun phrase

You can take this even further!

> The mad scientist, with wild, curly hair, strode purposefully into his cluttered laboratory, closing **the heavy oak door** loudly behind him.

In 21 words, we have built up a detailed picture of the scientist, the laboratory and the door.

We could keep on adding more details.

✓ Tip

Use your imagination to let you see what you are writing about. Then tell your readers everything about it. Make your descriptions really detailed.
- colour
- material
- size
- position

6   Grammatical words

Activities

1. Add two words to each of these phrases to make expanded noun phrases.
   a. the teacher
   b. some rabbits
   c. my sister
   d. his bike
   e. our school

2. Use the following prepositions to make expanded noun phrases about a building.
   a. opposite
   b. on
   c. behind
   d. against

3. Use the example below to build up a sentence containing an expanded noun phrase about an animal.
   - rabbits (noun)
   - the rabbits (noun phrase)
   - all of the rabbits in the area round my home (expanded noun phrase)
   - All of the rabbits in the area round my home seem to be grey. (sentence)

4. Write two sentences containing two expanded noun phrases about the following.
   a. a clown
   b. a film star
   c. a bus

5. Write a sentence containing three different noun phrases about: a boy, a book and his bedroom.

6. With a partner, make a list of three nouns. Share your list with another pair. Choose one of your lists and develop it into a sentence containing three expanded noun phrases.

Grammatical words 7

Verbs: present perfect and past perfect tense

Learn

What is the present perfect?

What is the past perfect?

The **present perfect** is used for an action that happened at an unspecified time in the past.

I **have been** to the theme park before.

The **past perfect** is used for something that happened before another action in the past.

Jack **had never been** to a live football game, before Saturday.

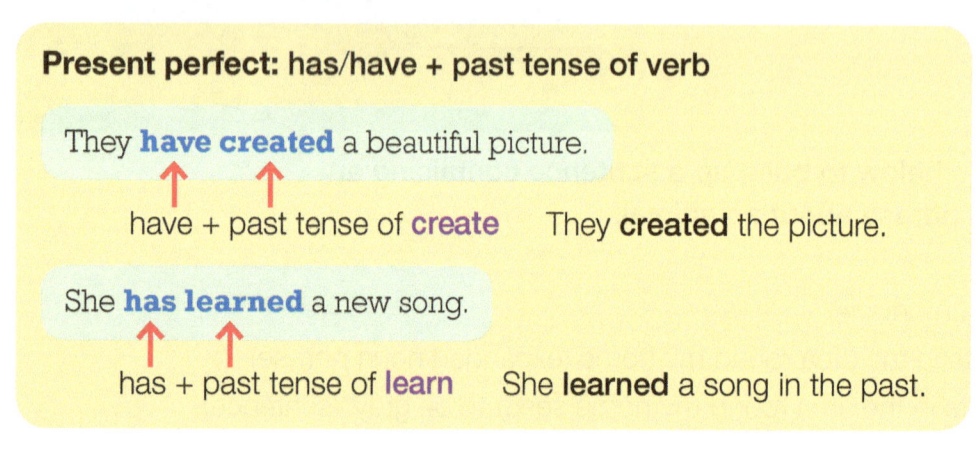

Present perfect: has/have + past tense of verb

They **have created** a beautiful picture.

have + past tense of **create**   They **created** the picture.

She **has learned** a new song.

has + past tense of **learn**   She **learned** a song in the past.

Past perfect: had + past tense of verb

We **had enjoyed** the meal, until **the bill arrived**!
   action 1   action 2

I **had seen** the dark clouds before **the rain came**.
   action 1   action 2

Key words

present perfect
past perfect

✓ Tip

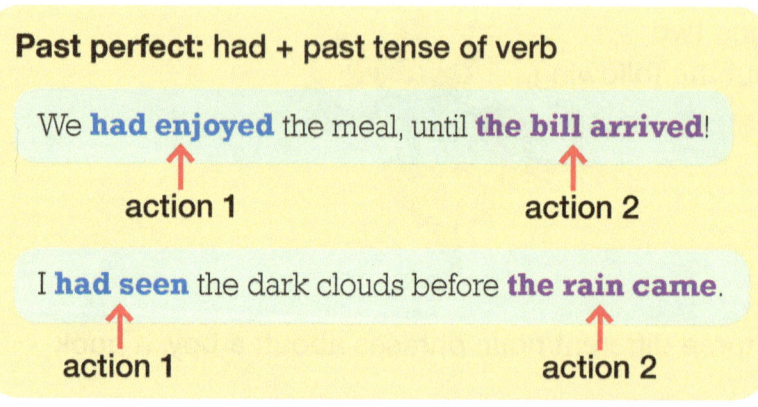

Perfect is a type of past tense. Don't be caught out by present perfect. It's still a past tense!

Activities

1. Complete the sentences using the present perfect of each verb in bold.

    a. **go**   He ____ out to play.

    b. **develop**   They ____ a method for baking perfect bread.

2. Rewrite this sentence using the past perfect form of the verb in bold.

    I **enjoy** the film until the end spoiled it.

Relative clauses

Learn

What is a relative clause?

A **relative clause** is a type of subordinate clause that adds information about a previous noun.

Relative clauses start with a **relative pronoun**.

> that   which   who   whom   whose   where   when

Relative pronouns introduce a relative clause and are used to start a description about a noun.

> The **man**, **whose car it was**, shouted angrily.
>
> **Relative clause**, starts with **whose**.
> Describes what the **man** owned. It modifies the noun.

Key words

relative clause
relative pronoun

> The **lioness**, **which was only two years old**, was used to being with people.
>
> **Relative clause**, starts with **which**.
> Describes the **lioness**. It describes the noun.

Relative clauses are often enclosed by commas. They start with a relative pronoun.

Activities

1. Write a relative clause for these sentences.

   a. The hotel, ____, was next to the beach.

   b. August, ____, is very busy.

2. Copy the table. Then put a tick to show the type of clause for the words in bold.

Sentence	Main clause	Subordinate clause	Relative clause
a. The rain, **which fell heavily**, made us cancel the trip.			
b. We called at Jacob's house **after we had seen Josh**.			
c. Unless you are able to pay tomorrow, **the trip will be full**.			

Grammatical words

Modal verbs

Learn

What is a modal verb?

Modal verbs are **auxiliary verbs** that change the meaning of other verbs. The modal verbs are:

| may   might   could   should   ought (to)   would   shall   can   will   must |

Least likely ←——————————————————→ Most likely

Modal verbs tell us how likely it is that something will happen.

Today is Monday so tomorrow **will** be Tuesday.

Modal verbs tell us how likely an action is:

1. Whether someone is able to do something: Isaac **can** play the guitar.

2. How likely something is: It **could** rain tomorrow.

They express degrees of certainty.

Must is more certain than **could**.   **Could** is less certain than **will**.

Learn these modal verbs:

We **must** be on time.   I **will** run quickly.   We **could** go swimming.

Activities

1. **Copy this sentence. Then underline the modal verbs.**
   We could stay in on Saturday night but we might go to the cinema instead.

2. **Choose the best modal verb to fit in this sentence and rewrite it.**
   George ____ improve his backhand if he wants to win the tennis match.

3. **Which of these events is most likely to happen? Write the sentence.**
   Emma will buy some jeans on Saturday.
   Emma should buy some jeans on Saturday.
   Emma ought to buy some jeans on Saturday.

Key words
auxiliary verb
modal verb

Adverbs of possibility

Learn

What is an adverb of possibility?

An adverb of possibility shows how certain we are about something.

These adverbs of possibility show we are sure of something happening.

definitely   certainly   obviously   clearly

These adverbs of possibility show we are less sure of something happening.

probably   perhaps   maybe   possibly

Maybe and **perhaps** usually come at the **beginning** of a sentence or clause.

Perhaps there will be ice cream for tea.
Maybe I can have a tablet for my birthday.

Other adverbs of possibility usually come in front of the main verb.

It is **clearly** going to rain.

However, they come after the verbs **am**, **is**, **are**, **was** and **were**.

It is **certainly** a busy road.

Activities

1. **Choose the best adverb of possibility for each sentence.**

    a. It is ____ six miles to town.

    b. I can ____ come to see you later.

    c. ____ we can have tea together?

2. **Explain how each adverb of possibility changes the meaning of the sentences below.**

    - We are clearly going to win this game.
    - We are possibly going to win this game.

Grammatical words   11

Subjects and objects

Learn

What are subjects and objects?

Every sentence has a **subject**.
The subject is the person or thing that does the action of the verb.

Many sentences have **objects** as well. The object has the action of the verb done to it. Objects are usually nouns, pronouns or noun phrases.

Let's look at an example.

I am selling.

This sentence has a subject but not an object. The verb is selling. **I** am doing the selling, so **I** is the **subject**.

I am selling **my bike**.

In this sentence **I** am still doing the selling, so **I** is still the **subject**.
My bike is being sold.
My bike is having the action of the verb done to it, so **my bike** is the **object**.

In a sentence:
- subjects usually come before the verb
- objects usually come after the verb.

Key words

subject
object

Activities

1. **Rewrite the sentence then circle the subject in each of them.**
   a. My mum drove the car.
   b. Our cat ate its food.

2. **Write the object in each of these sentences.**
   a. Dad is making tea.
   b. The dog chased the cat.

3. **Write the subjects and objects in each of these sentences.**
   a. You can ride your bike to school.
   b. Sadie sells shoes.
   c. Ronny, who is older than me, rides his motorbike to work.
   d. Mrs Burman, a very strict head teacher, runs her school well.

4. **Write these sentences with your own subjects and objects.**
   a. [Subject] threw the ball to [object].
   b. [Subject] scored three [object].
   c. [Subject] who lives at the end of our street, owns [object].
   d. [Subject], my best friend, sings [object].

Remember, subjects usually come before the verb. Objects usually come after the verb.

Active and passive verbs

Learn

What are active and passive verbs?

Active and **passive verbs** are different forms of verbs.

Most sentences use the active form of a verb. This means that the subject is doing the action and the object has the action done to it.

> **Kelly** has done the scoring, so she is the **subject**.
>
> **Kelly** scored all three **goals**.
>
> The **goals** do not do the scoring. They have been scored so they are the **object**.

When the **passive** is used, the object moves to the front and becomes the subject. The original subject moves to the end of the sentence but does not become the object. It becomes part of a **prepositional phrase** (you add 'by'). You also change the verb by adding 'was' or 'were'.

> **All three goals** has moved to the front of the sentence and becomes the subject.
>
> **All three goals were scored** by **Kelly**.
>
> The verb has **were** before it. **Kelly** has moved to the end of the sentence.

The passive form can be used in formal writing.

*To recognise the passive, look at the end of the sentence. It usually has **by** someone or something after the verb.*

Key words

active verb
passive verb
prepositional phrase

14 Grammatical words

Activities

1. Rewrite these sentences in the passive form.
   a. The chef made a wonderful meal.
   b. The police officer arrested the criminal.
   c. A mechanic mended our car.
   d. My cousin sent a letter to the Pope.
   e. Four mums from Yorkshire rowed a boat across the Atlantic Ocean in 2016.

2. Rewrite these sentences in the active form. Take care to make sure the subject and verb agree.
   a. A good time was had by everyone.
   b. The world record was smashed by the runner.
   c. Terrible floods have been caused by torrential rain.
   d. Many homes have been destroyed in America by a massive hurricane.
   e. Our cat was rescued from a tree by the fire brigade.

3. Read the following sentences with a partner. Decide whether each sentence is active or passive.
   a. The winning shot was made by Alisha.
   b. Our team won the league.
   c. Small mammals are hunted by eagles.
   d. Many people have climbed Mount Everest.
   e. The bird ate the worm.

Grammatical words 15

The subjunctive

What is the subjunctive?

Learn

The **subjunctive** is a form of the verb used in formal speech or writing.

The subjunctive uses only the simple form of a verb. For example, the simple form of **to run** is **run**.

The word **that** will help you to recognise the subjunctive. If the verb can be followed by **that** and something **should** happen, you will be using the subjunctive:

> **I demand that** you be quiet.

Subjunctives are used in different ways.

- **verb + that**

  to advise that   to ask that   to command that   to demand that
  to insist that   to propose that   to recommend that
  to request that   to suggest that

- **after phrases + that**

  it is essential that   it is desirable that   it is vital that

- **I, he or she + were**

  It is more natural to write **if I was to go to**, but this would be informal. The subjunctive form would be **if I were to go to**. This is known as the past subjective.

- **verb + that + be**

  I insist that you be here.

- When these verbs are followed by **that**:

  to advise   to propose   to recommend   to request
  to insist   to ask   to command   to suggest

  For example:

  > I insist that you be here.

- When these phrases are followed by **that**:

  it is essential   it is desirable   it is vital

  For example:

  > It is essential that you be on time tonight.

Subjunctives are only used in formal speech or writing. They are often used to suggest urgency or importance.

16   Grammatical words

Activities

1. **Rewrite these sentences, adding the subjunctive form of the verb in each sentence.**
   a. It is important that you **be/are** on time for the show.
   b. If I **was/were** you, I would take the risk.

2. **Find and copy the subjunctive in these sentences.**
   a. If I were to give you £25, what would you do with it?
   b. The teacher asked that her students be quieter.

3. **Rewrite these sentences in a formal style, using subjunctives.**
   a. If Zoe was to play instead of Zena, we'd win easily tonight.
   b. It is important that you are here on time.
   c. I wish it was Saturday.
   d. If only my car was more reliable.
   e. It is essential that pupils are polite.
   f. I advise that you are present at the hearing.
   g. Dr Lazarus asked that the patient waits outside.
   h. Chaz requested that Ziggy came to his party.
   i. It is essential that the referee is allowed to control the game.

Key words

subjunctive

Grammatical words

Commas to clarify meaning

Learn

How are commas used to clarify meaning?

Commas are placed in sentences to help us understand the meaning. Using commas within a sentence can help make the meaning clearer and avoid ambiguity.

Sometimes the meaning isn't clear without commas.

In the following sentences, the words are the same but the comma makes the meaning different.

"Let's eat Dad."

Someone is suggesting we should eat Dad!

"Let's eat, Dad."

That's clearer. Someone is telling Dad to eat.

The comma alters the meaning.

In the next two sentences, the commas alter the meaning again.

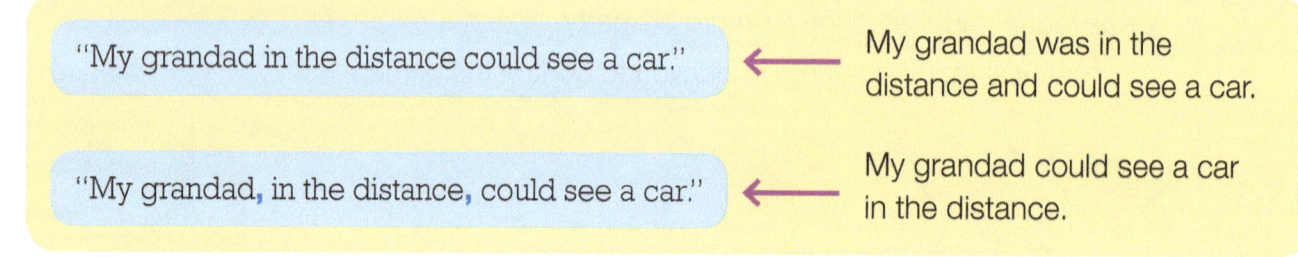

"My grandad in the distance could see a car." ← My grandad was in the distance and could see a car.

"My grandad, in the distance, could see a car." ← My grandad could see a car in the distance.

Activities

1. **Copy the sentences. Then put commas in the correct places to make the meaning clear.**
    a. My mum loves cooking my dad and me.
    b. Nate invited two boys John and Eddy.
    c. My uncle a singer and a dancer often appeared on television.
    d. Has the cat eaten Callum?

Question tags

Learn

What are question tags?

Question tags come at the end of a sentence. They try to make you agree with the sentence.

Examples of question tags include:

> isn't it?   don't you?   wouldn't you?

They are called **question tags** because they are tagged onto the end of a sentence. They make statements into questions.

You all want to go on the trip.
↑
statement

You all want to go on the trip, **don't you?**
↑
The question tag makes this into a question.

Not all question tags are negative.

No one wants to miss the trip, **do they?**   means the same as   You all want to go on the trip, **don't you?**
↑   ↑
positive question tag   negative question tag

Activities

A question tag always comes after a comma.

1. **Copy these sentences. Then you underline the question tags in these sentences.**
   a. You won't be late, will you?
   b. We're going to the cinema, aren't we?

2. **Add appropriate question tags to these sentences.**
   a. You'd like pizza for tea, ____?
   b. This is the right answer, ____?

Question tags are easy, aren't they?

Hyphens

Learn

What is a hyphen?

Hyphens are punctuation marks that are used to:
- join words together
- clarify meaning
- help pronunciation
- follow some prefixes.

Sometimes we join words together using a hyphen to show that they are linked.

> It was a **low-budget** film.

In this sentence, the film is neither **low** nor **budget**. We have to link the two words together to get **low-budget**, meaning it did not cost much.

The meaning of some sentences isn't clear without a hyphen.

> Joe Montana was a famous American football player.

The sentence is ambiguous. Was Joe a famous American who played football, or was he famous for playing American football? Adding a hyphen shows that Joe played American football.

> Joe Montana was a famous **American-football** player.

Without a hyphen, we would not know how to pronounce words like **re-enter**. The hyphen tells us that the letters on either side of it are both pronounced.

Here are some examples of when hyphens follow prefixes.

ex-police officer   **all**-inclusive   **self**-conscious

Key words
hyphen

Activities

1. Copy the sentences. Then insert hyphens to join the correct words together.

   My mother in law is coming for Sunday lunch.

2. Copy the sentences. Then insert a hyphen to make it clear that the **instruments have not been used much.**

   My uncle, a retired surgeon, showed me some of his little used instruments.

3. Rewrite 'resign' with a hyphen to show that it means 'to sign again'.

Bullet points

Why do we use bullet points?

Learn

Bullet points help you to structure writing.

They can be used in lists to present a lot of information in a short space.

There is a lot of information in this shopping list:

four bananas, a kilo of rice, some goldfish food, two litres of lemonade, 300g salt

It is easier to read when it has bullet points.

- four bananas
- a kilo of rice
- some goldfish food
- two litres of lemonade
- 300g salt

Sometimes the points in a list are hard to find because they get lost in the middle of it:

Happy Harry's haircuts are the talk of the town. Everyone wants one. You can get yours today.

Appointments are not needed.

Bullet points can make things easier to follow.

Happy Harry's haircuts:
- The talk of the town
- Everyone wants one
- Available today
- You don't need an appointment

Activities

1. Read the information about the two products below. Then make a bullet-pointed list of the important features of each one.

    a. **Morgan's Magic Medicine**
    Good for young and old alike, Morgan's Magic Medicine will cure your aches and pains. It works quickly and has no after-effects. It comes in handy half-litre bottles and is available from all good chemists.

    b. **Stop and Go bike locks**
    The handy little locks work like magic. Fitted to the front wheel of your bike they come on automatically every time you stop. They are so simple. No more hunting for keys or trying to remember codes. Just flick the switch and you're off again. Stop and go locks. They do what they say.

Punctuation 21

Colons and semi-colons in lists

Learn

How do you use colons and semi-colons in lists?

Colons introduce lists.

> To build this model tree you will need: glue, scissors, a ruler, tissue paper and some wire.

Semi-colons separate complicated items within a list.

> I had to buy a large loaf from the bakery; cheese and tomatoes from the deli; some onions, carrots and potatoes from the grocer; and some plastic plates from the hardware shop.

Activities

1. Copy these sentences. Then insert colons in the correct places.
   a. You will need to bring with you your passport, plane tickets, money, sun cream and sunglasses.
   b. We now know some countries that border the Mediterranean Sea Egypt, France, Spain and Italy.
   c. Warm waters can be found in the Mediterranean Sea, the Caribbean Sea and the Indian Ocean.

Key words
colon
semi-colon

✓ Tip

Remember, the colon is a link. It goes before the items in the list. Sometimes a semi-colon will be used when the items in a list already contain a comma.

2. Rewrite this bullet-pointed list as a sentence.

   I need to go to:
   - the supermarket for dog, cat and fish food
   - the heel bar to get my shoes, boots and sandals mended
   - the library to get some books for my history project.

✓ Tip

Sometimes semi-colons are links as well: they go between the items in a complicated list.

22 Punctuation

3. Rewrite these passages with colons in the correct places:

   a. The manager looked around the dressing room and said, "Some of you were useless last week, so for this week the defence will be Smith, Brown, Martin, Culshaw and Blair. In midfield I'm having Middleton, Sutton, Mason, Devlin. Up front it will be Nagla and Hussain."

   b. To succeed in life you need a lot of things talent, determination, hard work and a lot of luck.

4. Rewrite these lists with semi-colons in the right places.

   a. I have been learning Spanish on the internet for three weeks. Already I can: tell people my name book a room order drinks at the bar and explain that I do not understand a word they are saying.

   Remember the semi-colon before *and* in the last item in the list.

   b. I have bought all of the birthday presents for my family early this year. For my sister I have a camera and a memory card a box of expensive chocolates and a day at a spa. My mother is getting an imitation diamond necklace two tickets to the cinema, so she can take me as well and some chocolates. My brother is getting nothing because he is always mean to me never does his share of the washing up and plays Taylor Swift at full volume while I am trying to watch television.

5. Rewrite these passages with colons and semi-colons. Gaps have been left to show you where they should go.

   a. The head teacher looked at the boy and said, "Let's have a look at your attendance record. This is what you have done this week   Monday   morning absent   afternoon late. Tuesday   late in the morning   absent in the afternoon. Wednesday   absent morning   absent afternoon. Need I go on?"

   b. "From now on it's going to be like this   you will attend school every day   be on time   and make sure you are wearing your full uniform. Is that too much to ask?"

Separating independent clauses

> How do we separate independent clauses?

Learn

An independent clause needs a verb and a subject and can stand alone as a complete sentence. Some sentences have more than one independent clause. These can be joined together by colons, semi-colons or dashes.

Colons introduce a second clause that gives more detail to a first one. It shows there is a clear link between the two clauses but gives more emphasis to the second one.

> Mason was worried about asking Della out: he had struggled all day to find the right words.

Semi-colons link clauses of equal strength or importance.

> Tomorrow will be Friday; the day afterwards will be Saturday.

Dashes work like colons but are used in less formal writing.

> Your hair is so long it's getting in your eyes – it could do with cutting.

Activities

1. **Rewrite these sentences, combining each pair into one sentence with a colon in the right place.**
    a. Full marks in the test again. Just what I expected.
    b. Paris is a beautiful city. You can see many famous sights there.
    c. Martin didn't want to sell his car. He needed the money he would get for it.
    d. The sky looks dark. It will rain heavily all day.
    e. I love Skiathos. I am really looking forward to going there on holiday again.

2. **Add an independent clause to complete each one.**
    a. I know exactly what I want for my birthday:
    b. We are learning sign language at school:
    c. My brother is getting married next year:
    d. Before I tasted my soup I wondered if I had put too much salt in it:
    e. This year's school production is 'Oliver':

Key words
colon
semi-colon
dash

✓ Tip
Remember colons are used when the second clause tells you more about the first one.

3. Each of the following sentences has a star that should be a colon or a semi-colon to link independent clauses. Rewrite them with the correct piece of punctuation in place.
    a. My homework is due in tomorrow ★ I'll have to make sure I do it tonight.
    b. I was ten last year ★ this year I'll be eleven.
    c. I didn't do well in the spelling test this morning ★ there were some difficult words in it.
    d. Who dares wins ★ who doesn't dare loses.
    e. America is in the west ★ Russia is in the east.

4. Pick two of your answers and explain why you used a colon in one and a semi-colon in the other.

5. Why is the colon used in the sentence below?

    Two minutes of extra time to go and the score is 0–0: if someone doesn't score soon, we'll be going to penalties.

6. Rewrite the following sentences correctly by inserting either semi-colons or dashes. Compare your answers with a partner and discuss the reasons for them.
    a. Watch what you're doing ★ you could have had my eye out!
    b. The postman has just delivered a parcel I ordered ★ I was expecting it.
    c. Don't put it there ★ put it there!
    d. There is a really interesting programme about China on television tonight ★ it is the kind of thing I like to watch.
    e. All of my friends have phones ★ everybody uses them.

7. Which of these sentences is correct? Compare your answer with a partner. Write an explanation for your choice.
    a. The road is – difficult it's almost impassable – you'll need a strong vehicle.
    b. The road is difficult it's almost – impassable – you'll need a strong vehicle.
    c. The road is difficult – it's almost impassable – you'll need a strong vehicle.
    d. The road is difficult it's – almost impassable – you'll need a strong vehicle.

Parenthesis

Learn

What is parenthesis?

Parenthesis is the term used for a word, clause or phrase that is inserted into a sentence to provide more detail.
- Parenthesis is what is written inside **brackets**.
- **Commas** and **dashes** can do the same job as brackets.

Parenthesis does not make any difference to the understanding of the original sentence. It just gives the reader more information.

The following sentence gives a piece of information.

Key words
parenthesis
brackets
commas
dashes

> The Eiffel Tower is a very tall building.

By adding parenthesis, more detail is given but the meaning remains the same.

> The Eiffel Tower **(**which is in Paris**)** is a very tall building.

parenthesis with brackets

Commas and pairs of dashes can do the same job as brackets.

> The Eiffel Tower**,** which is in Paris**,** is a very tall building.

parenthesis with commas

Dashes tend to be used in less formal writing, such as in an email.

> The Eiffel Tower **–** which is in Paris **–** is a very tall building.

parenthesis with dashes

Remember, parenthesis is the information you add, not the punctuation around it.

26 Punctuation

Activities

1. a. Rewrite the following sentence, inserting the parenthesis using brackets.

> The three men talked quietly in the corner of the cafe.
> **Parenthesis:** *they looked like spies to me*

b. Rewrite the following sentence, inserting the parenthesis using commas.

> Denny is joining the army. **Parenthesis:** *my older brother*

c. Rewrite the following sentence, inserting the parenthesis using dashes.

> Suki won first prize at the dog show. **Parenthesis:** *a long-haired Alsatian*

d. Rewrite the following sentence, inserting the parenthesis using either brackets, commas or dashes.

> I had to keep very still while the doctor took my stitches out.
> **Parenthesis:** *who was very gentle*

e. Rewrite the following sentence, inserting Parenthesis 1 and Parenthesis 2 into the correct places using dashes and commas.

> The strongest wind ever will hit this country.
> **Parenthesis 1:** *a massive hurricane*
> **Parenthesis 2:** *probably on Tuesday next week*

Punctuation 27

Suffixes: 'ant' or 'ent'; 'ance' or 'ence'; 'ancy' or 'ency'?

Learn

Which suffix should I use?

To work out which **suffix** to use, it helps to know that some of them are related.

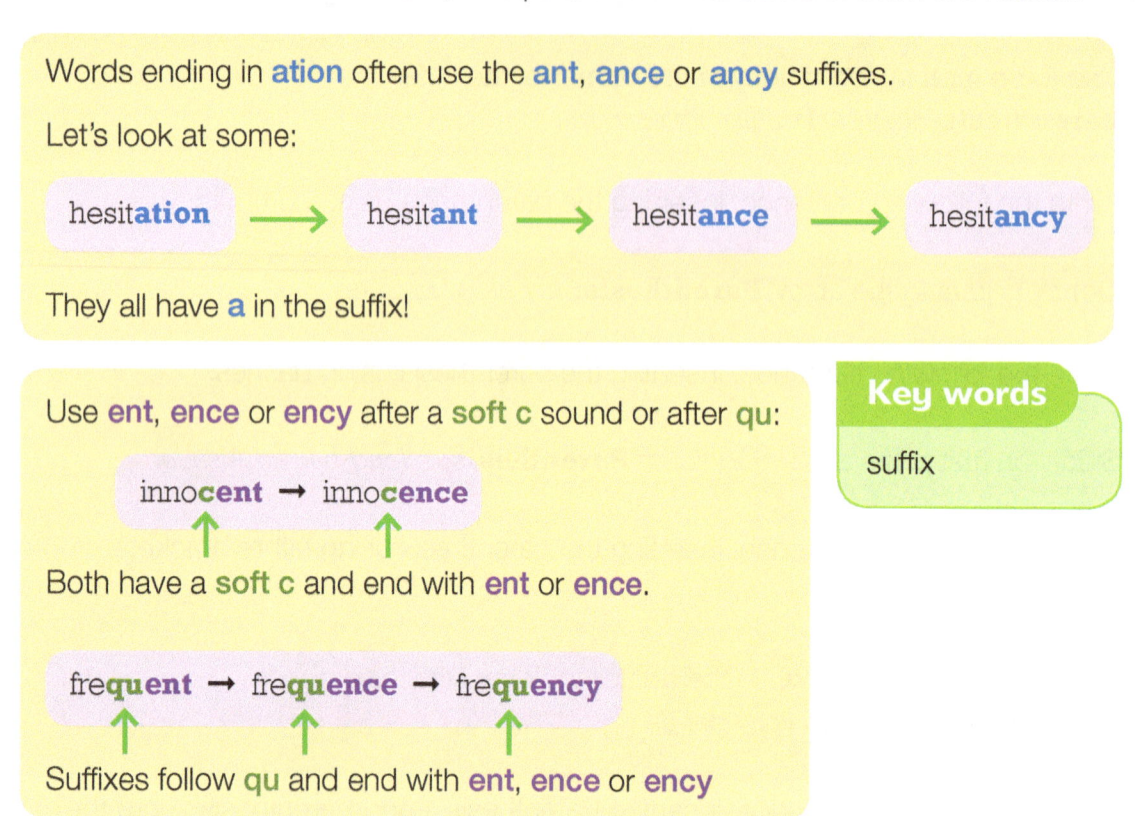

Words ending in **ation** often use the **ant**, **ance** or **ancy** suffixes.

Let's look at some:

hesit**ation** → hesit**ant** → hesit**ance** → hesit**ancy**

They all have **a** in the suffix!

Use **ent**, **ence** or **ency** after a **soft c** sound or after **qu**:

inno**cent** → inno**cence**

Both have a **soft c** and end with **ent** or **ence**.

fre**qu**ent → fre**qu**ence → fre**qu**ency

Suffixes follow **qu** and end with **ent**, **ence** or **ency**

Key words
suffix

There are words that don't follow these guidelines, which you need to learn.

For example: independ**ent** assist**ance**

If one of a word's suffixes has an **a** in it, other might: assist**ant** assist**ance**

Unfortunately, there are lots of words that don't follow these guidelines, and so you need to learn them! For example: independent, assistance. But, if one of a word's suffixes contains an **a**, they all will: assist**a**nt, assist**a**nce.

Vocabulary

Activities

1. Copy and complete each word choosing the correct suffix

Word beginning	'ent' or 'ant'
observ	
innoc	
toler	
obedi	

2. Write the correct spelling from each pair.
   a. buoyency/buoyancy
   b. hesitency/hesitancy
   c. agency/agancy
   d. accountency/accountancy
   e. consistency/consistancy

3. Write each sentence, choosing the correct spelling to complete it.
   a. The non-**existance/existence** of dodos in Mauritius has long been a cause for regret.
   b. Your help is more of a **hindrance/hindrence**.
   c. Please complete the **relevent/relevant** application form.

4. Use the words below in sentences.

   vacancy   redundant   efficiency   frequence   urgency

5. Find a fiction book. Copy these headings:

   ant   ance   ancy   ence   ence   ency

   How many words from your fiction book can you write under each heading?

Prefixes: 're', 'dis' or 'mis'?

Learn

The prefix **re** means again or back. It changes the meaning of the word.

regain — to gain **again**

redo — to do **again**

readjust — to adjust **again**

The prefix **dis** changes the word to its opposite meaning (often means not).

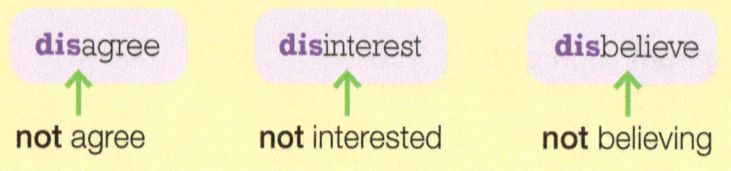

disagree — **not** agree

disinterest — **not** interested

disbelieve — **not** believing

The prefix **mis** also changes the verb to its opposite meaning (often to **do it badly**).

misuse — to use **badly**

mistreat — to treat **badly**

misbehave — to behave **badly**

Activities

1. Copy the lists below and draw lines to match the prefixes to the root words. Then write each new word.

    re   loyal
    dis   judge
    mis   design

2. Copy the table. Then use prefixes to change the meaning of these words so they match their definitions.

Word	New word	Definition
place		to put back again
calculate		to work out wrongly
tasteful		objectionable

Adding suffixes to words ending 'fer'

Learn

*How do I add a suffix starting with a vowel to words ending with **fer**?*

To add a suffix starting with a vowel to words ending **fer**.
- You double the end consonant if the final vowel is stressed.
- You do not double the end consonant if the final vowel is unstressed.

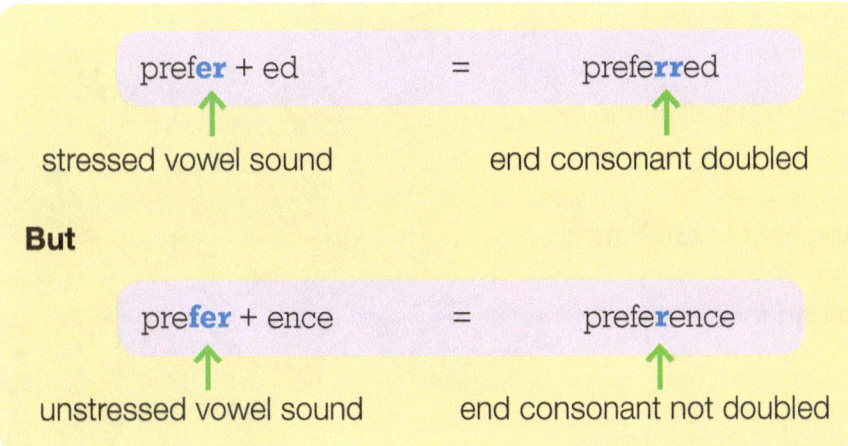

pref**er** + ed = prefe**rr**ed
↑ ↑
stressed vowel sound   end consonant doubled

But

pref**er** + ence = prefe**r**ence
↑ ↑
unstressed vowel sound   end consonant not doubled

Activities

1. Rewrite each sentence, choosing the correct word.
   a. The doctor was **refering/referring** him to a specialist.
   b. The head teacher wrote a glowing **reference/refference**.

2. Write each word with the correct ending.

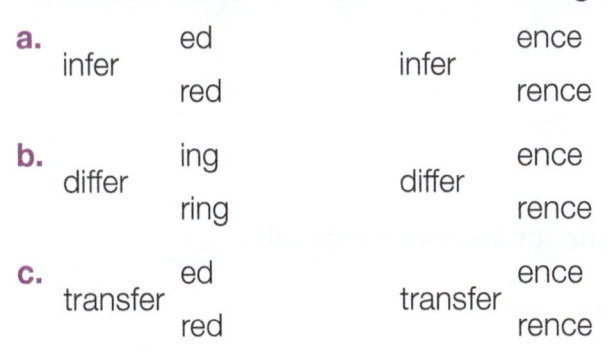

   a. infer — ed / red   infer — ence / rence

   b. differ — ing / ring   differ — ence / rence

   c. transfer — ed / red   transfer — ence / rence

Vocabulary 31

Synonyms

Learn

What are synonyms?

Synonyms are words with the same or similar meaning.

Using different synonyms for words can make our writing more interesting.

It is a **big** elephant.

Large, **enormous** and **massive** are all synonyms for **big**.

"That is an **enormous** elephant," **said** Ranvir.

The word **said** can be changed for a more interesting synonym:

declared   spoke   uttered   pronounced

✓ Tip

Can you think of some synonyms? When writing, ask these questions.
- What other words mean the same?
- Are they more interesting or precise?

Activities

1. Copy this list. Then tick all the synonyms for the word 'difficult'.

   complex   arduous   effortless   intricate   easy

2. Copy these words then draw lines to match each word to its synonym.

ancient	antique
curious	known
familiar	genuine
sincere	inquisitive

Key words

synonym

32 Vocabulary

Antonyms

Learn

What are antonyms?

Antonyms are words with the opposite meaning.

Using different antonyms can make our writing more interesting.

Light is the antonym of **heavy**.

It has the opposite meaning.

> backward ⟵⟶ forward
>
> Moving **forward** is the opposite of moving **backward**.
> **Backward** is the antonym of **forward**.

Here are some more examples of antonyms.

Word	Antonym
encourage	discourage
guilty	innocent
night	day
singular	plural

✓ Tip

Sometimes adding a prefix to a word can create an antonym.
- happy ⟶ **un**happy
- agree ⟶ **dis**agree

Activities

1. Copy the list and draw lines to match each word to its antonym.

   healthy   minimum
   young   mature
   permanent   unwell
   maximum   temporary

2. Choose an antonym to replace each word in bold.
   a. I **made** a massive tower.
   b. The successful man was very **humble**.
   c. The **foolish** child had no packed lunch.

Key words

antonym

Vocabulary 33

Informal and formal vocabulary

Learn

What is the difference between informal or formal vocabulary?

We use different vocabulary in different situations and in different kinds of writing. You probably wouldn't talk to your head teacher in the way that you would talk to your baby sister!

Formal vocabulary: is used in official documents or situations.

Informal vocabulary: is used in more personal documents when in relaxed situations.

Formal vocabulary	Informal vocabulary
Talking with people in authority	Talking with friends or family
Giving a speech in school	Asking for things in shops
Interviews	Diaries
News bulletins/weather reports	Notes
Letters of application for jobs	E-mails and texts

Formal vocabulary uses Standard English. It may use words and phrases that are specifically related to the situation, for example, in a courtroom.
Informal vocabulary may use slang. It may use simpler words.

Formal vocabulary	Informal vocabulary
discover	find out
request	ask for
enter	go in
our house	ours

✓ Tip

Decide what kind of written or spoken language you are using and who it is for. This will tell you whether to use formal or informal vocabulary.

Your meaning can be exactly the same using formal or informal vocabulary.

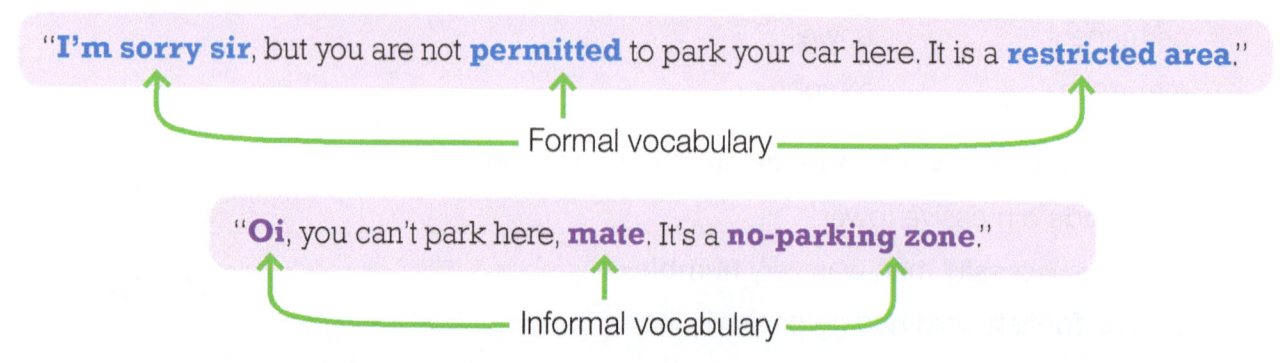

"**I'm sorry sir**, but you are not **permitted** to park your car here. It is a **restricted area**."
— Formal vocabulary —

"**Oi**, you can't park here, **mate**. It's a **no-parking zone**."
— Informal vocabulary —

34 Vocabulary

Activities

1. Which of these situations require formal vocabulary and which need informal?
   - A shopping list
   - A reply to a written wedding invitation
   - A presentation to your class
   - A telephone bill
   - A phone call to a friend
   - A postcard to your sister from your holiday

2. Complete this table. You may need to use a dictionary to help you.

Formal vocabulary	Informal vocabulary
commence	
conclude	
renovate	
beverage	

3. Rewrite this telephone conversation using formal vocabulary.

   Sonny: Yow Tezza, Sonny here!
   Tezza: Hi Sonny. Whatcha after?
   Sonny: You done that homework? It's rock hard.
   Tezza: Nah. I'm gonna do it afters. There's a sound proggy on the telly I wanna watch first.
   Sonny: Giz a bell when you do. I'm gonna put me feet up for a bit then have a go at it.

4. With a partner, write a playscript:
   a. in which a young person uses informal vocabulary to explain to his or her parent why they were late for school.
   b. Rewrite the playscript so that the young person uses formal vocabulary to explain the lateness to their head teacher.

5. With a partner, design:
   a. a flyer for a window-cleaning company
   b. headed paper for your school.

   You will need to decide whether to use formal or informal vocabulary.

6. Share your designs with another pair. Explain where and how you have used formal and informal language.

Vocabulary 35

Letter strings: 'ought'

Learn

What is a letter string?

A letter string is a group of letters that make one sound, within a word.

The letters **ought** can be used to make many different sounds.

These are the most common **ought** words.

ought	thought	bought	brought
sought	fought	nought	wrought

Learn the letter string **ought** and spelling these words will be easy.

This letter string makes an /**ort**/ sound.

However, in dr**ought** these letters make an /**out**/ sound (as in shout).

Activities

1. **Choose the best word to go in each sentence.**

   brought   bought   sought   wrought

   a. They ____ a way out of the forest, but it was hard to find.
   b. I ____ some toys with me.
   c. They installed a new ____ iron gate.
   d. We ____ some cakes to have with our sandwiches.

2. **Copy the words and draw lines to match the words to their definitions.**

   ought   nothing
   fought   considered
   nought   struggled
   thought   should

✓ Tip

Be careful: some words have the same sound but are spelled differently; for example, **caught** and **court**, **taught** and **taut**.

Letter strings: 'ough'

Learn

What sound does the letter string **ough** make?

The letter string **ough** makes several sounds: /**uff**/ (as in stuff); /**off**/; /**oo**/ (as in moon); /**oe**/ (as in toe); and /**ow**/ (as in cow).

Using the letter string **ough** can be tricky because it can make so many sounds. Here are some examples of each sound.

'uff' (as in cuff)	'off'	'oo' (as in moon)	'oe' (as in toe)	'ow' (as in cow)
rough	cough	through	though	bough
tough	trough		dough	plough

Some **ough** words don't belong in these groups:

thorough   borough

These words both have an /**uh**/ sound at the end.

✓ Tip

Say the word, then work out which sound it makes.

Activities

1. Use these 'ough' words to make new words to fit in each space.

   dough   rough   tough

   a. They ____ worked out how to make the model.
   b. The doors were made of ____ glass.
   c. We bought some ____ to eat at the fairground.

2. Write the 'ough' words to match each definition.

Definition	Word
area	
branch	
cultivate	
sufficient	
animal food container	

Silent letters

Learn

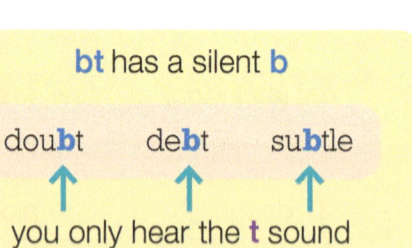

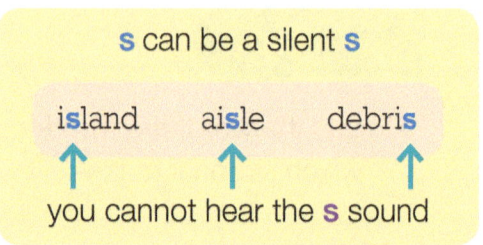

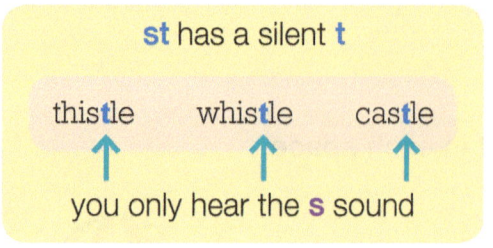

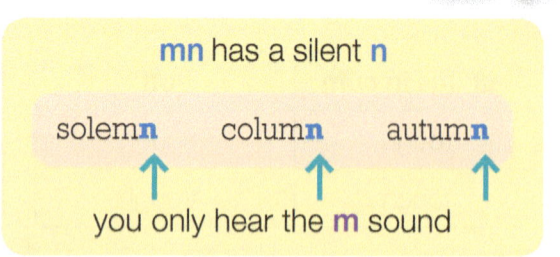

When are silent letters used?

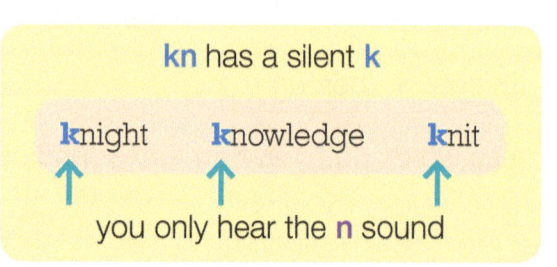

Silent letters are used to write a sound – but you can't hear them when you say the word.

There are lots of silent letters. They often pair up with another letter.

bt has a silent **b**

dou**b**t   de**b**t   su**b**tle

you only hear the **t** sound

mn has a silent **n**

solem**n**   colum**n**   autum**n**

you only hear the **m** sound

s can be a silent **s**

i**s**land   ai**s**le   debri**s**

you cannot hear the **s** sound

kn has a silent **k**

knight   **k**nowledge   **k**nit

you only hear the **n** sound

st has a silent **t**

this**t**le   whis**t**le   cas**t**le

you only hear the **s** sound

Activities

1. **Underline the silent letter in each word in bold.**
   a. They went over the bridge to the **Isle** of Anglesey.
   b. Look at the third **column**.
   c. We are **indebted** to you, thanks to all your efforts.
   d. Caitlin saw a **mistle** thrush in the garden.

2. **Write the correct spelling for each word.**
   a. dought/doubt/dout
   b. isle/iall/iel
   c. condam/condemn/condem
   d. brissle/brissel/bristle

✓ Tip

To help you spell a word, pronounce it with the silent letter: **sub–tle**. If you can hear each letter, you will use it when writing the word.

'c' or 's'?

Learn

What kind of sound can **c** and **s** both make?

c and **s** can both be used to make a soft **s** sound (as in sun).

How do we know when to use **c** or **s** at the start of a word?

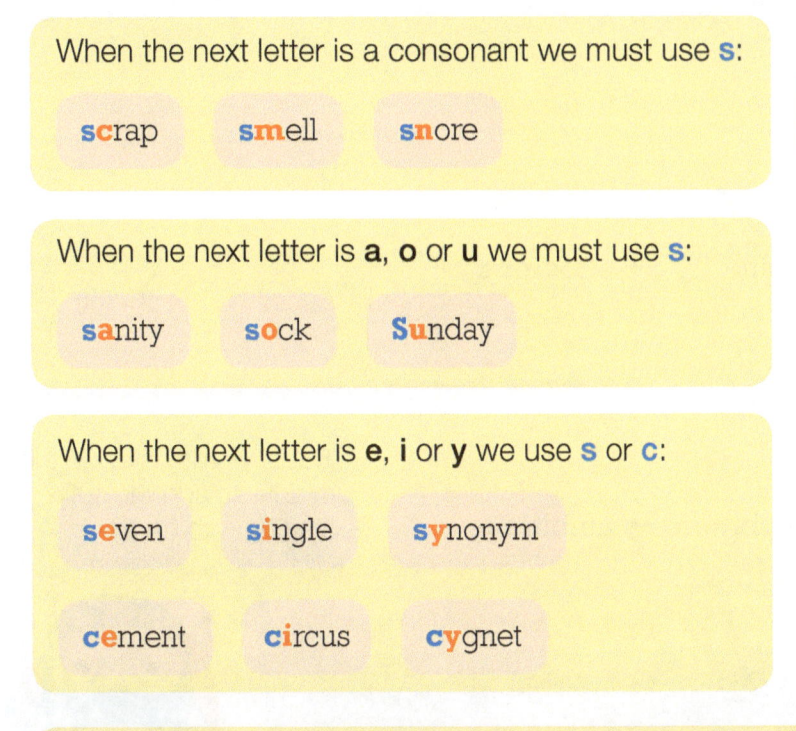

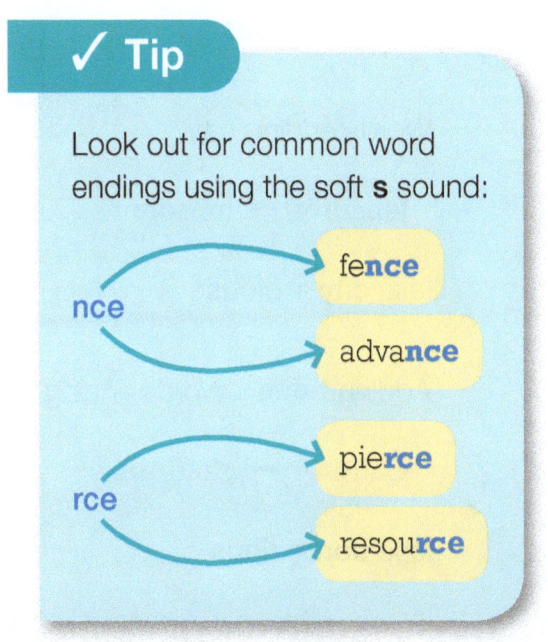

When the next letter is a consonant we must use **s**:

scrap   **sm**ell   **sn**ore

When the next letter is **a**, **o** or **u** we must use **s**:

sanity   **so**ck   **Su**nday

When the next letter is **e**, **i** or **y** we use **s** or **c**:

seven   **si**ngle   **sy**nonym

cement   **ci**rcus   **cy**gnet

✓ Tip

Look out for common word endings using the soft **s** sound:

nce → fe**nce**
nce → adva**nce**

rce → pie**rce**
rce → resou**rce**

After a short vowel sound in short words we use **ss**:   ki**ss**   mi**ss**   che**ss**

In longer words, we use **ice**:   prejud**ice**   precip**ice**   off**ice**

f**ace**   sp**ace**   r**ace**   all use **ace**.

Activities

1. Rewrite the sentences using the correct spelling of the words in bold.
   a. I went **twice/twise** to call on Ahmed.
   b. There was a very **fierse/fierce** dog behind the gate.
   c. It was **bliss/blice** sitting in the hot sun.
   d. Our teacher **cuggested/suggested** that we read books by Michael Morpurgo.

2. Write the correct spelling of the word in bold.
   a. Our doctor's **practiss** is very busy.
   b. I asked for a **peese** of lemon cake.

Spelling 39

Adding 'cious' or 'tious'

Learn

When do I add **cious** or **tious**?

Adding cious Words ending **ce**

vi**ce** → vi**cious**   gra**ce** → gra**cious**

lose **ce** + **cious**

Words ending city

tena**city** → tena**cious**   atro**city** → atro**cious**

lose **city** + **cious**

Adding tious Words ending **tion**

Cau**tion** → cau**tious**   ambi**tion** → ambi**tious**

lose **tion** + **tious**

These words have **t** in the middle so add the suffix starting with **t** = **tious**

✓ Tip

There are exceptions to these rules such as, **fiction – fictitious**

Activities

1. **a.** Choose the correct suffix to make a new word.

   | cious   tious |

   malice   infection   space   nutrition

   b. Use each new word in a sentence.

2. **Write the correct spelling of each word.**
   a. cautous   cauteous   cautious
   b. suspisious   suspitious   suspicious
   c. delicious   delicous   deliceous
   d. consciencious   conscientious   consciencous

40 Spelling

Adding 'tial' or 'cial'

Learn

When do I add **tial** or **cial**?

cial is often used after a vowel.

off**ial**   sp**ecial**

tial is often used after a consonant

confide**ntial**   influe**ntial**

BUT there are exceptions:

initial – **tial** after a vowel
financial – **cial** after a consonant.

Some exceptions: initial, financial, commercial, provincial.

You will need to learn the exceptions to the rule!

Activities

1. **Work with a partner. Dictate these sentences to your partner.**

   - The torrential rain prevented them from walking.
   - The artificial flowers did not look like real flowers.
   - My favourite martial art is judo.

   Now highlight any spelling mistakes. Can your partner work out how they should have been spelled?

2. **Work with a partner. Ask your partner to dictate these sentences to you.**

   - The official accident report was released yesterday.
   - The social club has a disco on Saturday.
   - Katie has the potential to be an excellent swimmer.

   Now highlight any spelling mistakes. Can you work out how they should have been spelled?

3. Look at the 'tial' and 'cial' words in the above sentences. Write the words into columns under the headings: 'tial' or 'cial'.

Spelling 41

Adding 'able' or 'ably'

Learn

When do I add **able** or **ably**?

The **suffixes able** and **ably** are usually used when it is possible to hear the complete **root word**, first.

The suffixes **able** and **ably** are common.

afford + able = afford**able**   afford + ably = afford**ably**
                                        — you can hear the root word

advis**e** + able = advis**able**   advisabl**e** + ably = advis**ably**
↑   — you can hear the root word
lose final **e**

manag**e** + able = manag**eable**   manage + ably = manag**eably**
                                        — you can hear the root word
need final '**e**' to make
soft /**g**/ sound

Activities

1. **Add the suffix 'able' to these verbs.**
   admire
   measure
   tolerate
   depend

2. **Add the suffix 'ably' to these verbs.**
   enjoy
   change
   rely
   reason

If **able** is added to words ending **ce** or **ge**, keep the final **e** to make a soft **c** and soft /**g**/ sound.

3. **What is the rule for adding 'able' or 'ably' to words ending in 'y'?**
   rely + able   rely + ably

Key words
suffix
root word

42 Spelling

Adding 'ible' or 'ibly'

> When do I add **ibly** or **ably**?

Learn

The suffixes **ible** and **ibly** are usually used when you cannot hear the complete root word.

The **ible** and **ibly** suffixes are not as common.

neg**lect** + ible = **negl**ible

↑ lose final syllable   ↑ you hear only part of the root word

comprehen**d** + ibly = comprehen**s**ibly

↑ change final letter   ↑ you hear only part of the root word

Not all words obey the rule!

forc**e** + ible = forcible

↑ lose final **e**   ↑ you can hear the root word

Activities

1. Copy and complete the root words, adding the suffixes 'ible' and 'ibly'.

Root word	+ ible	+ ibly
leger		
sense		
reverse		
defend		

> You may need to change part of the root word.

2. Rewrite each sentence, filling in the missing word ending with 'ible'.

   a. The burnt pie was totally ____.
   b. His writing was ____.

3. Rewrite each sentence, filling in the missing word ending with 'ibly'.

   a. The burglars had ____ entered the property.
   b. The child was ____ upset after the fall.

'ei' after 'c'

Learn

When do I use **ei** after **c**?

You use **ei** after **c** when it makes an /**ee**/ sound! (as in f**ee**d).

perc**ei**ve   rec**ei**ve

ei used after **c** to make an /**ee**/ sound.

Be careful: In many words **i** comes before **e**: achieve

When **ei** does not come after the letter **c**, it usually makes an /**ay**/ sound: reign, neigh.

Activities

1. Write the sentences, using the correct word from the box to complete them.

   | ceiling   receipt   received   conceived |

   a. I searched everywhere for the ____ so I could return the faulty game.
   b. The ____ was very uneven and would need plastering.
   c. The team finally ____ a plan which would help them win the tournament.
   d. Jack ____ a parcel on his birthday.

2. Write the correct spelling for each word.
   a. wiegh/weigh
   b. decieve/deceive
   c. field/feild
   d. perceive/percieve
   e. neighbour/nieghbour
   f. concieted/conceited

3. Write an explanation for each question.
   a. When does **ei** make an /**ee**/ sound?
   b. When does **ei** make an /**ay**/ sound?

44 Spelling

Tricky words

Learn

What is a tricky word?

A tricky word may have:
- several **syllables**
- an unusual spelling pattern.

You may need to split longer words into parts, or syllables, to make them easier to spell.

> **house**: one syllable   **prejudice**: three syllables
>
> Soft /**g**/ sound: is it **g** or **j**?   Soft /**s**/ sound: **ice** or **iss**?

Key words

syllable

- Break the word into syllables (parts).
- Say each part of the word slowly and clearly.
- Then work out how to spell each syllable.

Some words have sounds that could be made in different ways.

> Ask: **a** or **e**?   **sion** or **tion**?
>
> expl**a**na**tion** = four syllables
>
> Try writing it each way. Which looks best?
> Say the word clearly and you can hear the **a**.

Breaking a word into syllables and then working out how to spell each part makes it easier. Try the different ways of making tricky sounds. Which looks best?

Activities

1. **Copy the words then shade each syllable in a different colour. Describe the tricky bits in each word.**

    a. immediately

    b. necessary

2. **Write the correct spelling for each word.**

    a. government   goverment   guverment   governmeant

    b. marvelous   marvelus   marvellus   marvellous

    c. wrecognise   reckognise   recognise   reconise

Look at a word you misspell. Write the word correctly. Highlight the tricky bit and memorise the correct spelling.

Spelling 45

Homophones

Learn

What is a homophone?

A **homophone** is a pair of words that sound the same but are spelled differently.

There are lots of homophones. Here are a few examples.

principal → the leader

principle → a belief

prophet → someone who foretells the future

profit → a financial gain

I awoke early this **morning**. → the start of the day

They are in **mourning** following the king's death. → in sorrow (following a death)

license → (verb) to allow

They were **licensed** to fish on this part of the river.

licence → (noun) a permit which allows you to do something

My television **licence** has expired.

stationary → not moving

The car was **stationary**. (Think: There is **ar** in c**ar** and station**ar**y!)

stationery → office paper/envelopes and materials

I ordered some more **stationery** for the office.

(Think: stationery includes paper. There is **er** in pap**er** and station**er**y!)

✓ Tip

Can you find an easy way to remember what a pair of homophones mean?
For example: **here** or **hear**. Hear has **ear** hiding in it!

Activities

1. **Copy the sentences and underline the correct homophone for each sentence.**
   a. We **heard** / **herd** the firework display in the park.
   b. I wondered **whose** / **who's** car was parked outside my house.
   c. The burglar tried to **steel** / **steal** the television, but it was very heavy.
   d. The porridge was **two** / **to** / **too** hot!

2. **Write a sentence for each homophone.**
   a. passed   past
   b. guessed   guest

3. **Explain the meaning of each homophone.**
   a. aloud   allowed
   b. farther father
   c. waste   waist

4. **Write the other homophone for these words.**
   a. great
   b. dissent
   c. cereal
   d. bridal

Key words

homophone

Spelling 47

Using dictionaries

Learn

How do I use a dictionary?

Dictionaries are great tools but you need to know how to use them.

Checking spelling

You might not know how to spell some words but will often know how they start. Use the first three or four letters of a word to check spelling.

The key to finding your way around a dictionary quickly is to know the alphabet.

Dictionaries are organised in alphabetical order, with words starting with **a** at the beginning and words starting with **z** at the end. After that, they are arranged by the order of their second letter. Words that start with the same second letter are then arranged in the alphabetical order of their third letters, and so on. It sounds complicated so here is an example from one section of a dictionary. In this example, all of the words begin with **p**.

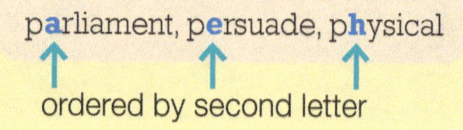

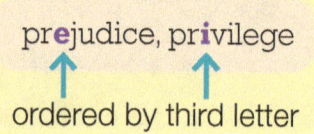

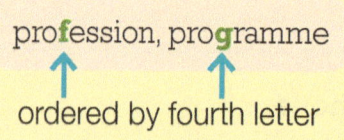

p**a**rliament, p**e**rsuade, p**h**ysical
↑ ↑ ↑
ordered by second letter

pr**e**judice, pr**i**vilege
↑ ↑
ordered by third letter

pro**f**ession, pro**g**ramme
↑ ↑
ordered by fourth letter

To start using a dictionary, you just need to know what letter the word you want starts with. The more letters you know at the start of the word, the easier it is.

Checking meaning

Sometimes you need to check the meaning of some words to make sure you are using the right ones.

Except and **accept** sound and look very similar. A dictionary will help you to tell the difference.

Except: preposition – meaning a person or thing that is not included in a statement which has just been made. For example, *Our car was easy to find because every car in the car park was blue* **except** *ours.*

Accept: verb – meaning to take something that is offered. For example, *I decided to* **accept** *my dad's offer of a lift to school.*

Dictionaries also tell you word types.

If you look up **hand**, the dictionary will tell you it could be a *verb*, as in 'to hand something to someone', or it could be a *noun*, as in 'the part of your body at the end of your arm'. This is useful when you use a thesaurus as it helps you choose the correct word to fit the meaning.

48 Spelling

Activities

1. Rewrite these words in the order you would find them in a dictionary.

   > definite   government   achieve   rhyme   bargain   category
   > language   frequently   embarrass   necessary

2. Rewrite these words in the order you would find them in a dictionary.
   Use the first two letters of the words to help you.

   > amateur   mischievous   committee   rhythm   recommend   marvellous
   > determined   correspond   cemetery   dictionary   restaurant   accommodate

3. Rewrite these words in the order you would find them in a dictionary.
   Use the first three or four letters of the words to help you.

   > needle   need   newer   necessary   neither   net
   > nest   neat   neon   nettle   never   network

4. Find a word in the dictionary that starts with 'dis' and means *to take someone's attention away from what they are doing*.

5. Rewrite the following words with either a 'c' or an 's' at the beginning.
   Then look them up in a dictionary to see if you were right.

   > ircle   ervice   ircus   urvive   ease   iren

6. Use a dictionary to check which of these words have the correct spelling.

   > farewell   mischievious   neccessary   neice   neither   piece   tomorrow

7. Use a dictionary to help you choose the correct word in these sentences.

   a. I will be going away next **week/weak**.

   I will have to sit down as I am feeling **week/weak**.

   b. I have to sit down as I am feeling **feint/faint**.

   He made a **feint/faint** move that sent me in the wrong direction.

   c. That is not **allowed/aloud**.

   Don't speak **allowed/aloud**.

8. Look up 'hand' in a dictionary. How many different meanings can you find?
   Use one of the meanings correctly in a sentence.

Spelling   49

Using a thesaurus

Learn

How do I use a thesaurus?

A thesaurus is a really useful tool. It helps you to find other words that have similar meanings to ones you are using. This means you don't have to use the same word twice.

A thesaurus is organised in alphabetical order, just like a dictionary. After that the words are arranged by the order of their second letter. Words that start with the same second letter are then arranged in the alphabetical order of their third letters and so on. It sounds complicated so here is an example from one section of a thesaurus. In this, all of the words begin with 'i'.

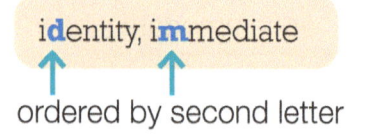

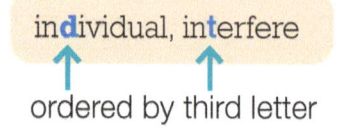

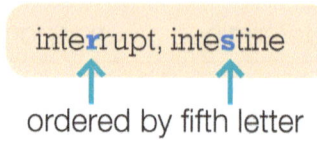

i**d**entity, i**m**mediate   in**d**ividual, in**t**erfere   inte**r**rupt, inte**s**tine

ordered by second letter   ordered by third letter   ordered by fifth letter

To start using a thesaurus, you just need to know what letter the word you want starts with. The more letters you know at the start of the word, the easier it is.

Checking meaning

A thesaurus is not a dictionary. They do different jobs. A thesaurus does not tell you what a word means. It only gives you words with similar meanings. These are called **synonyms**. However, because some words have more than one meaning, a thesaurus might give you words that don't fit into what you are writing.

Sometimes you need to check the meaning of some words in a dictionary to make sure you are using the right ones.

In this sentence the word **right** means correct.   That is the **right** answer.

✓ **Tip**

Looking up **right** in a thesaurus would give you: *correct, accurate, true, precise, just, proper, entitlement, privilege, permission* and lots more. You might have to look some of these words up in the dictionary to make sure you picked the best word.

If we try some of the words in the example sentence, they don't work.

That is the privilege answer – doesn't make sense.
That is the precise answer – makes sense.
So do *correct, accurate, true* and *proper*.

Try putting your new word in your sentence to see if it make sense. Make sure the word you use fits with your meaning.

Activities

1. Rewrite these words in the order you would find them in a thesaurus.

   environment   existence   especially   exaggerate   equip   excellent   embarrass

2. Choose one of the following words. Look up its synonyms in a thesaurus and write them down.

   sacrifice   secretary   shoulder   signature

3. Write a sentence using your chosen word from the question above. Then rewrite it using one of the words from your thesaurus.

4. Replace *conscience* in this sentence with a word from a thesaurus.

   Going to war was against his conscience.

5. Replace *familiar* in this sentence with a word from a thesaurus that shows Izzie always writes this way.

   Izzie signed the birthday card in her familiar style of handwriting.

6. Use a thesaurus to find another word to replace *familiar* in the same sentence. This time make it mean that Izzie is writing in an informal style.

7. Write as many words as you can think of that mean the same as *friend*. Use a thesaurus to check how many you got right.

8. A thesaurus sometimes gives you words that mean the opposite of the one you are using. These are called 'antonyms'. Use a thesaurus to find antonyms for: *ancient, definite, desperate, hindrance, individual.*

Spelling 51

Identifying main ideas

Learn

What does identifying main ideas mean?

The main ideas are the important things that the author wants the reader to know.

Often there will be only one main idea in a passage but there may be more than one paragraph.

Don't worry about each individual idea. Look for something that links them all.

In the passage below there is one main idea.

> The house at the end of our street is very spooky. It is painted black and has tall, thin chimneys. All of the windows are dark and no one ever seems to go in or out.

Each of the sentences is about something different but they are all about the spooky house at the end of the street, so this is the main idea.

When you identify something, you find it in a passage. To find the main ideas, decide what a passage is about overall.

✓ Tip

Try reading the text and then thinking of a **heading** that fits it overall.
- There are sentences on the colour of the house, what it looks like and who goes there. None of these is the main idea.
- Each sentence is about what makes the house spooky. So the title could be '**The Spooky House**'.

Activities

Highlight the words in each sentence that show what the sentence is about. Then find a link between them.

1. **Read this passage and identify the main idea.**

   > People have always been fascinated by the moon. Is it made of cheese? What is on the other side of it? Can human beings live there? Modern science has answered many of these questions and we now know that there is much more to learn about the moon than we already know.

Identifying key details

What does identifying key details involve?

Learn

- Identify means find.
- The main ideas are the important things that the author wants the reader to know.
- The key details are what the author writes about the main ideas.

Start by identifying the main idea or ideas.

> The city of Hull sits proudly on the north bank of the River Humber. At one time, it was the biggest fishing port in the country but now its fishing fleet has disappeared. Nowadays, it is a modern city with fast motorway access and direct ferry links to Europe.

Main idea: how Hull has changed.

Next, highlight the points that tell us more about the main idea.

> The city of Hull sits proudly on the north bank of the River Humber. At one time, **it was the biggest fishing port in the country** but now **its fishing fleet has disappeared**. Nowadays, it is a **modern city** with **fast motorway access** and **direct ferry links to Europe**.

Each point tells us something different.

Now, use your highlighted points to give three ways that Hull has changed.

1. It is a modern city.
2. It has fast motorway access.
3. It has direct ferry links to Europe.

Activities

1. Read the passage below.

   > Last summer we had our best holiday ever. We went to Menorca and spent a week splashing about in the pool and on the beach. We laughed all day and never had to worry about going to bed late or getting up early. I made lots of new friends.

   a. What is the main idea?
   b. Give two key details from the text to support this:

Reading 53

Summarising main ideas

Learn

What does summarising ideas mean?

Summarise means sum up. When you summarise, you say briefly what the passage is about.

A summary might be one word, a complete sentence or more than one sentence. You need to find ideas from the whole text.

You have to read the whole passage before you can summarise. In the passage below, there are different ideas for each paragraph.

> My sister Carly is very kind. She has a mischievous twinkle in her eyes. She is very popular and makes every day feel like a party.

Main idea: my sister Carly

> My other sister, Caroline, is very different. She is a very private person who prefers her own company. She has a good sense of humour but rarely uses it outside of the house.

Main idea: my sister Caroline

There are sentences about two sisters. The link between these two ideas (or paragraphs) are linked by the differences in the sisters.

When there is a lot of information in a passage, you might have to write more than one sentence as a summary.

The main idea in the following passage is healthy eating. The reasons that support healthy eating have been highlighted in **blue** and the reasons against it are in **orange**.

> **Healthy eating**
>
> Everybody loves food. Children love fast food. **Burgers, chips and nuggets all taste great**. There are lots of takeaway shops, meaning that **fast food is easy to buy**. **It isn't always good for you** though. Lots of **fast food contains large amounts of salt and fat. Salads are really healthy** but **some people think that they are boring**. **Healthy eating gives us energy and makes us grow strong**. However, if you're busy, **a takeaway once in a while won't do you too much harm**.

Highlight the key details and then write them in a table like the example below.

Reasons against healthy eating	Reasons that support healthy eating
Burgers, chips and nuggets all taste great.	Fast food isn't always good for you.
Fast food is easy to buy.	Fast food contains large amounts of salt and fat.
Some people think that salads are boring.	Salads are really healthy.
A takeaway once in a while won't do you too much harm.	Healthy eating gives us energy and makes us grow strong.

Then use the table to help you write a summary. Concentrate on the main points.

> Fast food is easy to get and it tastes great. It isn't always good for you because of what it contains. It's important to eat healthy foods like salads but a takeaway occasionally won't harm you too much.

Activities

1. Read the passage below. Write the main ideas for each paragraph.

   a.
   > On our street there are three takeaway shops. There is an Indian, a Chinese and an Italian pizza place.

   b.
   > We have a different meal every Saturday night. My favourites are lamb rogan josh, chicken chop suey and garlic bread.

2. Sometimes, the summary is in the form of a heading or subheading. Write which of the following do you think the best heading for the passage above would be?

   > Favourite food   Saturday night takeaway   Our street   Fast food

3. Read the passage below. Highlight the key details and then write a summary.

   > My mother paints pictures. She is really good at landscapes. She's done great pictures of the sea, mountains and lakes. Her portraits aren't as good but she is working on them.

Reading 55

Retrieving and recording information

Learn

- Retrieve means find.
- Record means write down.

What does retrieving and recording information mean?

Read the following passage. Key pieces of information have been highlighted.

> **The *Titanic***
>
> The *Titanic* has captured the imagination of the public more than any other ship in history. Perhaps it is because it was **described as 'unsinkable'** by its designer. Perhaps it is because it **sank on its first voyage**. Perhaps it is because there is so much **mystery** surrounding its loss. Whatever the reason, there has been continuous interest in the *Titanic* for **over a hundred years**.

Example questions

What are the reasons people have been interested in the *Titanic*?

is the same as:

Why have people been interested in the *Titanic*?

Some questions will ask you to join information together. For example, in this case, you might be asked to **draw lines to link the *Titanic* to why people might be interested in it.**

Look for the other key words in the question: these tell you what to retrieve from the text. In this question they are: 'interested in the *Titanic*'.

Scan the text above and you'll find three reasons.

Titanic	It is a famous ship.
	→ It was said to be unsinkable.
	→ It sank on its first voyage.
	→ There is so much mystery about it.
	It sank over a hundred years ago.

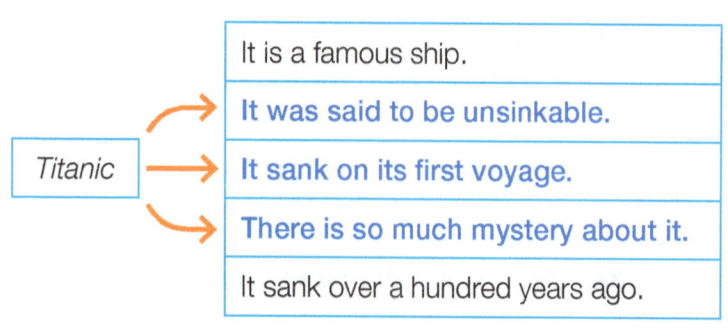

Look for the first key words in the question: **why**, **what**, **who**, **where**, **when** or **how**.

Key words

retrieve
record

✓ Tip

Look closely to find the answers.
- **Why** = find a reason
- **Who** = find a name
- **Where** = find a place
- **When** = find a time
- **How** = find an explanation
- **What** can be any of the above.

Activities

1. **Read 'The *Titanic*' again.**
   a. Who is interested in the *Titanic*?
   b. How long is it since the *Titanic* sank?
   c. Why would people be surprised that it sank?
   d. Interest in the *Titanic* has been:

   > increasing   reducing   continuous   overwhelming

   Remember to look for the key words. They tell you what to retrieve.

2. **Read the continuation of 'The *Titanic*'.**

   > Nowadays the *Titanic* lies at the bottom of the Atlantic Ocean. It is still recognisable as the wonderful ship it once was, even though it is encrusted with barnacles and sea life. Instead of the rich and the famous, it is now home to a whole host of different sea creatures. There are memorials to the *Titanic* in Belfast, Liverpool, Southampton, Washington DC and New York. Although there is still huge interest in it, it will probably never be brought to the surface.

   Copy the table below and draw lines to link the *Titanic* with information about it nowadays.

Titanic	It is at the bottom of the Pacific Ocean.
	It looks just like it did before it sank.
	Sea creatures now live in it.
	There are memorials in five cities.
	It will be raised soon.

Making comparisons

Learn

What does making comparisons mean?

Comparisons show us what is similar or different in a text.

Read the following passage.

> **My favourite birds**
>
> My hobby is bird watching, or ornithology, to give it its proper name. Why have two names? Well, it's a bit like the birds themselves. They all have common names but they also all have proper names. Did you know that sparrows are also called *Passeridae*? No? Neither did I until I started watching them.
>
> I don't really like little birds. My favourites are the hunting birds. I love owls. They are so graceful. They fly in silence, seemingly without effort. Some people don't like them at all. They see them as cruel hunters. They prefer birds that don't even fly, like penguins, but they hunt too. People like the awkward way they walk. What's the point in a bird that can't fly? It's like a fish that's scared of water.

Give one reason why people might like owls and one why they might not.

> Like owls: They are graceful or they fly in silence, seemingly without effort.
> Dislike owls: They are seen as cruel hunters.

Read the continuation of the passage.

> Owls glide through the air in pursuit of their prey. Penguins can't fly but they do the same underwater. An owl in flight is a graceful sight. Penguins are equally graceful in the water. Owls hop while penguins walk. Neither bird is particularly comfortable on the ground but, of the two, penguins are more suited to being on land. Owls can be found in the wild all over the world but penguins only live in the southern hemisphere.

To compare, you have to show the similarities and the differences.

Comparison	Owls	Penguins
Similarities – movement	Graceful in flight	Graceful in water
Differences – movement	Hop	Walk
Differences – where they live	All over the world	In the southern hemisphere

Activities

1. Read the continuation of the 'My favourite birds' passage again.
   a. Give one thing that is different between owls and penguins.
   b. Give one thing that is similar between owls and penguins.

2. Read the following passage.

   > Some animals are more popular than others. For instance, cats are almost universally liked while snakes are hated the world over. I am perfectly happy to have my cat slide onto my knee and settle down to watch television with me. I can't say the same of a snake. Why? Cats are much more familiar to us, so their danger seems less. Cats do not hunt large prey, like us. Snakes? Well, what do we know? They hiss and spit, but so do cats when they are annoyed. Snakes hunt small animals. So do cats.

   Don't get yourself tied up in knots. To compare just show similarities and differences.

   a. Compare the author's attitude to cats and snakes.
   b. What is similar between cats and snakes?
   c. What differences are there between cats and snakes?

   Find the key words in the question and look for them in the text.

Reading 59

Themes and conventions

Learn

> What are themes and conventions?

- Themes are ideas that run throughout the text.
- Conventions are the things that help you know what type of writing it is.

This table shows you some themes and conventions.

Type of writing	Possible themes	Convention of this type of writing
Poetry	love, war	verses, rhyme, rhythm, figurative language
Drama	relationships	speech without inverted commas, stage directions
Fiction	myths and legends, adventure, love, war, good and evil, loss, fear, danger, rich and poor, strong and weak, wisdom and foolishness	heroes and heroines, villains, frightening situations, cliff-hangers, 'good' winning, using stock locations and characters – dark woods and wicked witches
Non-fiction	history, geography, celebrities, sport, gossip, cars and lots of others	textbooks, magazines/newspapers, brochures, headings, subheadings, facts, pictures, columns, bullet points, numbers and dates

You need to be able to identify themes and conventions, and comment on them.

> So you need to be able to say how a text is written.

In the passage below, the clues to the **theme** have been highlighted.

> Only another minute left! Karine's hands **fumbled with the fuse**. If she cut the wrong wire, **it would be the end for all of them**. Which wire? **Karine didn't know!** Thirty seconds. She had to choose one. A 50–50 chance. **Red. No green!** Fifteen seconds! **This was it.** Karine would have to cut one now. **She held the green wire and hoped!**

All of the highlighted words are typical of language you would find in action stories. The time countdown increases the excitement. These are **conventions**. This is different to the **main idea** because in this paragraph the main idea would be about defusing a device, which is part of the themes of action stories about spies or war.

60 Reading

The theme of the passage below is danger. The clues that identify this have been highlighted.

> **Stranded** high on the ledge, Elliott knew **he was in trouble**. His **leg was broken** and his **radio had been lost** in the fall. Above him, a layer of ice **threatened** to drop down at any moment. He could feel himself **slipping slowly towards the edge**. It was only **a matter of time**.

To comment on the theme, explain what it is.

> **For example:** It follows the tradition that the hero faces immediate death. Everything suggests that he cannot survive. The ending makes us think that he will slide over the edge to his doom.

To comment on the conventions, show how they help the reader understand the theme.

> **For example:** The text is an adventure story. It has many of the usual elements, including a dangerous location, an injured hero and seemingly inevitable destruction.

Activities

To help identify the theme, highlight the ideas that go throughout the passage.

1. What is the main theme in this passage?

   > Dorca the dragon flew across the night sky. Her quest was to find the secret of eternal dragon life. She knew that the knights of Nemore would try to stop her but she had dragon magic on her side!

2. Read the passage again.
   a. Find and copy a phrase which shows that the above passage has this theme.
   b. Explain how your phrase or sentence fits this theme.
   c. Give two ways that the extract uses the conventions of your chosen theme.

Fact and opinion

Learn

What is fact and opinion?

- A **fact** is true and can be proved.
- An **opinion** is what someone thinks or believes.

You need to be able to tell the difference between facts and opinions.

In the passage below, there is one **fact** and one **opinion**.

To tell if something is a fact, ask: 'Can it be proved?'

> **Jessica Ennis-Hill won a gold medal in the heptathlon at the London Olympics in 2012.** She is the most talented heptathlete Britain will ever have.

- Jessica Ennis-Hill did win the Olympic gold medal. **Can this be proved? Yes.** There is video evidence to prove it.
- She is the most talented…will ever have. **Can this be proved? No.** Nobody knows what will happen in the future. The text makes it seem as if Jessica is the most talented heptathlete. How? It starts with a fact which proves that she is a top-class athlete and therefore implies that she is the most talented. We might believe the second sentence is a fact because we know that the first one is, but there is no way we can predict the future and what new heptathletes Britain will have.

Read the following passage.

> The tallest mountain in Wales is Mount Snowdon. It is known in Welsh as *Yr Wyddfa*.

How many **facts** are in the passage? **Two.** Both sentences contain **facts** that can be proved.

> **At 1085 metres high, Yr Wyddfa** is the highest mountain in Wales. You can walk to the top or, for the less energetic, there is the Snowdon Mountain Railway.

✓ Tip

Watch out for **foggy phrases**. They're hard to see through and it's easy to get lost in them! For example, 'Everybody knows' and 'There can be no doubt' are foggy phrases. They make things seem like **facts** when really they are **opinions**.

Activities

Read the following passage.

> I think that the *Mona Lisa* is a strange picture. Painted by Leonardo da Vinci and also called *La Gioconda*, it is kept in the Louvre in Paris. It is only 77cm by 53cm and is hung in a dark room to avoid the light damaging it. When I went, the room was packed with people trying to see the picture. It was not awe-inspiring. The statue of *Venus de Milo* is much more impressive. It's not worth queuing to see the *Mona Lisa*. You'd be better off spending your time in the Egyptian section. The sphinx in there is really impressive.

1. Copy the table. Then put a tick in the correct box to show whether each of the following statements are fact or opinion.

	Fact	Opinion
a. The *Mona Lisa* is 77cm by 53cm.		
b. The *Mona Lisa* is a strange picture.		
c. The *Mona Lisa* is not awe-inspiring.		
d. The *Mona Lisa* is in a dark room.		

> Sentences that include 'I think' or 'I believe' are opinions. Don't be fooled. Remember, facts can be proved.

2. Find and copy three facts from the passage that are not included in the table above.

3. Find and copy three opinions that are not included in the table above.

Reading 63

Explaining and justifying inferences

Learn

- Inferences are assumptions that you make from clues in the text, like how a character is feeling or why something happens. They are the bits the writer doesn't actually tell you but that you can work out for yourself.
- Explain means say what you think.
- Justify means give reasons for what you think, using parts of the text to prove your points.

What does explaining and justifying inferences mean?

OK, so it means read between the lines, work out what is happening and show us why you think that.

Explaining inferences
Some parts of the text below have been highlighted. These are the clues.

Charlie was **really fed up**. **His day had already been bad** and he had a feeling that **it was about to get a whole lot worse**.

→ The author has told you how Charlie is feeling and why. The only thing to infer is what has made his day bad but there aren't any clues to help you.

Charlie came in from school. He **threw his bag** into the corner, **sighed loudly** and **kicked the bin**.

→ The author has not told you how Charlie is feeling or why. You have to infer that he is unhappy. The clues are in his actions. We still don't know why he is unhappy though.

1. What do the clues in the second part of the text tell us?
   Charlie is behaving badly.
2. What do the clues not tell us?
   Why Charlie is behaving badly.
3. What inference can we make?
   Charlie is unhappy.

Justifying inferences
You need to give reasons for your thoughts. To do this you need proof. This comes from the clues. In the second part of the text, the three clues that you can use as evidence have been highlighted.

Ask yourself: 'What has happened and how do we know?'

What has happened to make Charlie unhappy?

The author has not told us but we can **infer** from the first sentence that something has happened at school to make Charlie unhappy.

You could try to make inferences about this but it is much more difficult as there isn't any evidence.

Writing answers

Write down an inference that you can make from the passage.

> Charlie is unhappy because of something that has happened at school.

Explain an inference that you can make from the passage.

> When Charlie throws his bag into the corner, sighs loudly and kicks the bin, he is showing he is unhappy. He has just come in from school so it is likely that something has happened there to upset him.

Find and copy two phrases from the text to support your inference.

1. threw his bag
2. sighed loudly

Remember to prove what you think.

Activities

1. **Read the following passage and answer the questions.**

   > Ella went as slowly as she could into the hall. She wished she had been ill that morning. The maths test was about to take place. The test papers were lying menacingly on the desks. As Ella sat down, she could feel her heartbeat increasing. She wished she had practised more. She took a deep breath and turned the paper over.

   a. How do you think Ella is feeling at the start of the passage?
   b. Find and copy a phrase that supports your thoughts.
   c. Do you think Ella will do well in the test?
   d. Use evidence from the text to support your thoughts.

Predicting what might happen

Learn

What does predicting mean?

When you predict, you say what you think is likely to happen. Usually you have to give reasons for your ideas. These come from clues that are written in the text.

I see. You have to read the story and say what you think will happen next. This is like being a detective.

Look at this sentence.

The **fire alarm** sounded.

To predict what would happen next, you have to look for the clues in the text. In this case, the clue has been highlighted. The fire alarm has gone off so what happens next must follow on from that. It has to be realistic, possible and likely. So it is no use predicting that an elephant will arrive, suck up water from a pond and then blow it down its trunk to put the fire out!

The following passage ends with the same sentence. Look at the highlighted clues to help predict what might happen next.

Mia had left the classroom to go to the toilet. On the way back she could smell **burning**. It was coming from a **store room**. Mia pushed the door open carefully and saw the **flames**. She **shut the door** quickly. **Her teacher and her classmates were in the next room**. She had to get them out. She punched the red button on the wall. The **fire alarm** sounded.

What happens next?

It would be realistic, possible and likely that the teacher and the children would all leave the building. By closing the door, Mia has made sure that the fire won't spread quickly, so that should enable the fire brigade to arrive in time to put it out.

66 Reading

Read this passage. The last sentence is different.

> Mia had left the classroom to go to the toilet. On the way back she could smell burning. It was coming from a store room. Mia pushed the door open carefully and saw the flames. She shut the door quickly. Her teacher and her classmates were in the next room. She had to get them out. She punched the red button on the wall. Nothing happened!

How does changing the ending change your prediction?

You can't keep the same prediction anymore because the clue in the last sentence tells you that something else will have to happen if everyone is to be saved. This gives you a much wider choice of possible predictions.

Activities

1. **Read this passage.**

   > Mia hit the button again. Still nothing! She knew she mustn't panic. She ran down the corridor to her classroom and raced inside.
   >
   > "The store room is on fire!" she shouted.
   >
   > Mrs Milner took control. She told the pupils to leave everything on their desks and to go out of the building as quickly as possible. She made sure everyone had left the classroom and followed them. As she went outside she pressed the red button by the door. The fire alarm sounded.

   a. What is likely to happen next?
   b. Explain why you think this is likely.

   Only highlight the points that give clues about what might happen. Use them to make your prediction.

2. **Read this passage.**

   > Once the fire was out, the chief fire officer wanted to talk to Mia. She did not know why. He interviewed her in the head teacher's office. When he spoke his tone was very serious.

   a. Give two predictions about what the chief fire officer might have wanted to talk to Mia about. You should use information from the whole story in your answer.
   b. Use evidence from the text to explain your answers.

Words in context

Learn

What are words in context?

Words in context means how words are used in a particular passage.

Read the following information from a text about eagles.

> There can be few more exciting sights than that of an eagle plummeting towards the earth in pursuit of its prey.

You may not know what *plummeting* means so read the whole sentence again. The eagle is moving towards the earth. Therefore, *plummeting* has to be telling us **how** the eagle was moving. It is in 'pursuit of its prey' so it has to be moving quickly.

Which of the following does the word *plummeting* mean in this sentence?

> descending   diving   sliding   tumbling

In this case, you should pick *diving* as it fits with 'in pursuit of its prey'.

The other answers all link with 'towards the earth' but they do not give the feeling of speed.

Activities

Read the following passage.

> The cliff was uneven. Slowly, bit by bit, hand over hand, I clambered up it.

1. *I clambered up it.*

   Which of these words has a similar meaning to 'clambered' in this sentence?

   > walked   climbed   raced   looked

If you don't know what a word means, try to work out what the whole sentence means and see if that gives you any clues.

Exploring words in context

Learn

What does exploring words in context mean?

Explore means to go into the meaning of the words.

To explore, you have to look at a range of possible meanings of a word or phrase. You may need to read the whole sentence or paragraph again, and then work out what the word means.

Read this sentence.

> The price of bread has rocketed in the last five years.

What does 'rocketed' mean in this sentence?

The clue is in the word. What do rockets do? They move quickly; they soar upwards; they go sky-high.

To explore the use of 'rocketed', you would need to explain **how** and **why** it is being used in the sentence. In this context, 'rocketed' has been used to show how quickly the price of bread has gone upwards because it reflects the speed of the rise.

Now you have to look at how the words are being used as well.

✓ Tip

If you're not sure what a word means in a sentence, read the sentences on each side of it.

Activities

Read this passage.

> I do not like rice pudding. There are few foods that I detest more. I avoid it if possible.

1. *There are few foods that I detest more.*

   Which of these words means the same as 'detest' in this sentence?

   | hate   want   love   need |

   Explain why you have chosen your answer.

Try all of the words and see which one makes most sense when you read the complete sentence.

Reading 69

How writers use language

Learn

How do writers use language?

Writers use language to have an effect on the reader through:
- vocabulary used
- use of different sentence types and links between them
- different types of text (fairy stories, newspapers, magazines, letters).

You have to write about the effect each has on the reader.

Always explain why and how the language that is used affects the reader.

Words

Different words show different shades of meaning. Some words like **nice** or **good** are very vague and give the reader little idea of what they mean. **It was a scary film** could cover anything from **mildly creepy** to **bloodcurdlingly terrifying**. Choosing words carefully is important to ensure that readers know exactly what writers are trying to say.

Sentences

Different forms of sentence create a response in the reader.

- **Everybody loves ice cream.** This is a **statement**. It seems to be a fact but is it? Actually, it's not a fact but it is presented as one so the effect is that the reader believes it is true.
- **Who can argue that Britain is the best country in the world?** This is a **rhetorical question**. It tries to make the reader agree with it by suggesting that no one could argue against it.
- **Finish ahead. Foot flat on the floor! Maximum speed. Go! Go! Go!** These **short sentences** have the effect of making the action seem fast, almost like a series of photographs.

Text

Texts are written for different purposes. You need to be able to identify the purpose and show how the writing fits it. This one is written to inform.

This includes you!

Use of **us** and **you** makes it seem like the writer is talking to the reader

Everyone needs to exercise. Exercise makes **us healthier** and can help **us live longer**. It can help **us feel better** and **reduce weight**. **You** could **walk**, **jog**, **run** or **swim**. **These are cheap** and they will all make a huge difference to **your** health. For further information, visit **www.healthierlife.com**

Reasons to exercise are highlighted: *makes us healthier*, *live longer*, *feel better*, *reduce weight*

More information

Place to find more information

Gives information and choices: *walk, jog, run* or *swim*

Activities

1. The following questions are about the Exercise extract.

   a. Give four reasons why we should exercise.

   b. Name two forms of exercise that are recommended.

   c. *These are **cheap** and they will all make a **huge** difference to your health.* What is the effect on the reader of the words in bold?

2. Read this passage.

   > Run! Run like your life depends on it – because it does.
   > Run! Don't look back! Run! You'll know when to stop.

Language used	Effect of language
a. *Run!*	What is the effect on the reader of repeating *Run!*
b. *because it does*	What is the effect on the reader of this phrase?
c. *Don't look back!*	How does this sentence increase the tension or excitement in the passage?

✓ Tip

For this question, you have to show which words and writing techniques have been used and what the effect is on the reader.

Reading 71

Enhancing meaning: figurative language

Learn

What is figurative language?

Figurative language is **imagery** used by writers to create word pictures that help the readers see what is happening and enhances the meaning.

- Examples of this include **analogy**, **metaphors**, **similes**, **personification**, **assonance** and **alliteration**.
- You need to write about the effect of the figurative language.

Some of the figurative language has been identified in this passage.

> Waves **lapped** in **mournful murmurs** against the wreck of the *Free Choice*. The ship lay, **a broken-backed corpse**, across the reef. Stranded in shallow seas, the vessel **groaned like a ghost** as each wave hit it.

Figurative language	Type of language	Explain the effect
lapped	**Personification** – because the waves don't really have tongues	Lapped means 'licked'. The description of the action of the waves makes us think about the movement.
mournful murmurs	**Alliteration** – it creates an effect by repeating consonant sounds, in this case the **m**	Alliteration helps the reader hear the noise.
a broken-backed corpse	**Metaphor** – it compares more strongly, usually using **is** or **was**. The metaphor also uses **personification** to help the reader picture the ship	This metaphor helps us imagine how damaged the ship looks.
groaned like a ghost	**Simile** – it compares by using 'like' or 'as' **Alliteration**	The simile compares the groaning to a ghost, which makes the description more vivid.

It's important to know the name of the figurative language but it's even more important to say what its effect has been.

72 Reading

Activities

1. Read the following passage.

   > My brother had broken my favourite toy. I roared like a monster in anguished anger. Tears burned my eyes. My mother, hearing my cries, held me like a nurse until I stopped sobbing. My father brought the remedy – superglue.

   a. *I roared like a monster…*

      Which of these words does the sentence above contain.

      | a metaphor   alliteration   personification   a simile |

   b. In the table below, highlighted in italics, are examples of figurative language from the passage. Copy the table, then in each case, state what type of figurative language is used and explain its effect.

Language used	Type of language and effect
Tears *burned* my eyes	
held me *like a nurse*	
My father brought the *remedy – superglue.*	

Key words

figurative
language
imagery
analogy
metaphors
similes
personification
assonance
alliteration

Features of text

Learn

What are features of text?

- Language features – the way the words are used.
- Structural features – the way the text is organised.
- Presentational features – the way the text looks.

Here are some examples of different features.

Language features	Structural features	Presentational features
• Figurative language • Short/long sentences • Variety/repetition of words • Specific choice of words • Rhetorical questions	• Chapters • Table of contents • Headings and subheadings • Paragraphs or verses	• Pictures and captions • Diagrams • Columns and charts • Text boxes • Fonts and colour

In the following passage, a number of language, structural and presentational features have been identified for you.

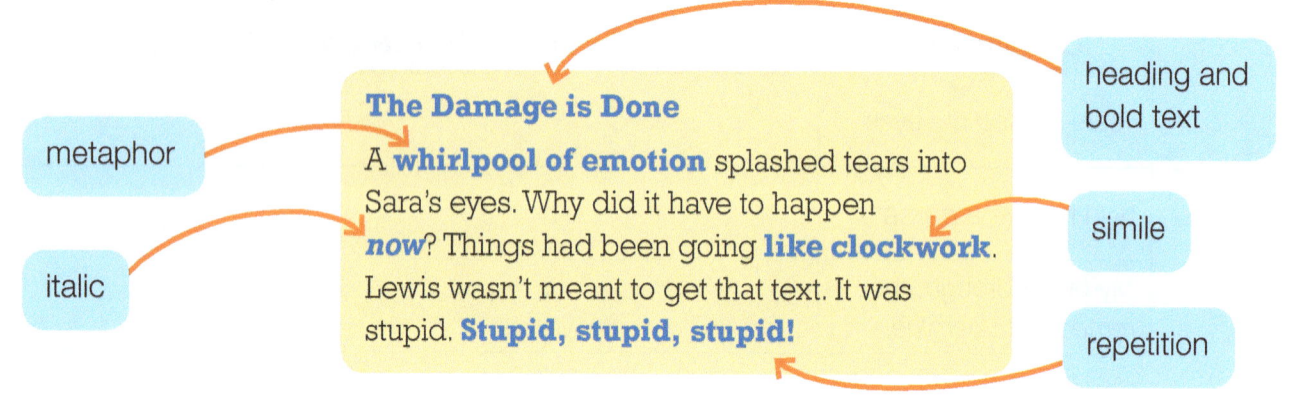

The Damage is Done

A **whirlpool of emotion** splashed tears into Sara's eyes. Why did it have to happen *now*? Things had been going **like clockwork**. Lewis wasn't meant to get that text. It was stupid. **Stupid, stupid, stupid!**

- metaphor
- italic
- heading and bold text
- simile
- repetition

Activities

Why oh why?

Sara stared at her phone. Why had she hit the *send* button?

1. Copy the table below and find and copy examples of language, structural and presentational features from the above text.

Feature	Feature name	Example
Language		
Structural		
Presentational		

74 Reading

Text features contributing to meaning

Learn

Text features are the language, structural and presentational features of texts. You need to explain how they help the reader understand the meaning of the text.

How do text features contribute to meaning?

This is the continuation of **The Damage is Done**. Some features are highlighted.

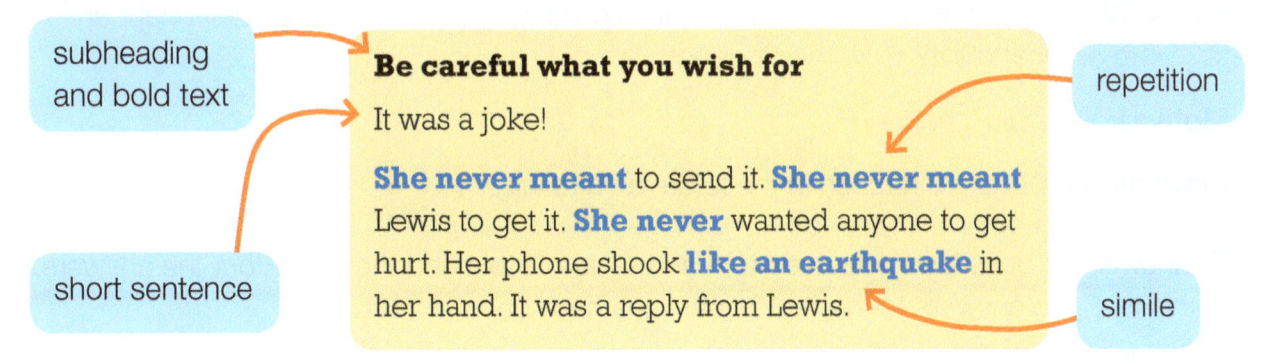

subheading and bold text → **Be careful what you wish for**

It was a joke!

She never meant to send it. **She never meant** Lewis to get it. **She never** wanted anyone to get hurt. Her phone shook **like an earthquake** in her hand. It was a reply from Lewis.

short sentence | *repetition* | *simile*

You need to be able to explain how each feature works in the passage as a whole.

Feature	What it does	Explanation
Subheading	Makes it easy to read	Breaks up the text and gives a summary of the main idea of the paragraph
Bold text	Draws attention to important text	Makes it stand out
Short sentence	Increases pace of text	It tells us more about what Sara was doing in a short space of time
Repetition	Reinforces point	Emphasises how little Sara had wanted the events to take place
Simile	Helps the reader imagine the scene	An earthquake is a huge disaster; that is what Sara is expecting when the text comes in

Activities

1. Read both parts of 'The Damage is Done'.
    a. How does writing in the third person help the reader?
    b. How does the writer build up tension in the following sentence?
        It was a reply from Lewis.

Reading 75

Asking questions

Learn

Why do we ask questions?

We ask questions to improve understanding and to help us give reasons for our thoughts.

> Types of questions to ask include:
>
> **Facts:** **What** has happened? **Where** was it? **When** was it? **Who** or what did it happen to? **Who** or what did it? **How** was it done?
>
> **Motives:** **Why** did it happen?
>
> **Predictions:** **What** will happen in the future as a result?

To answer the questions, you need to read the whole text and then work out the answers. In this text, the answers to the **facts** questions have been labelled.

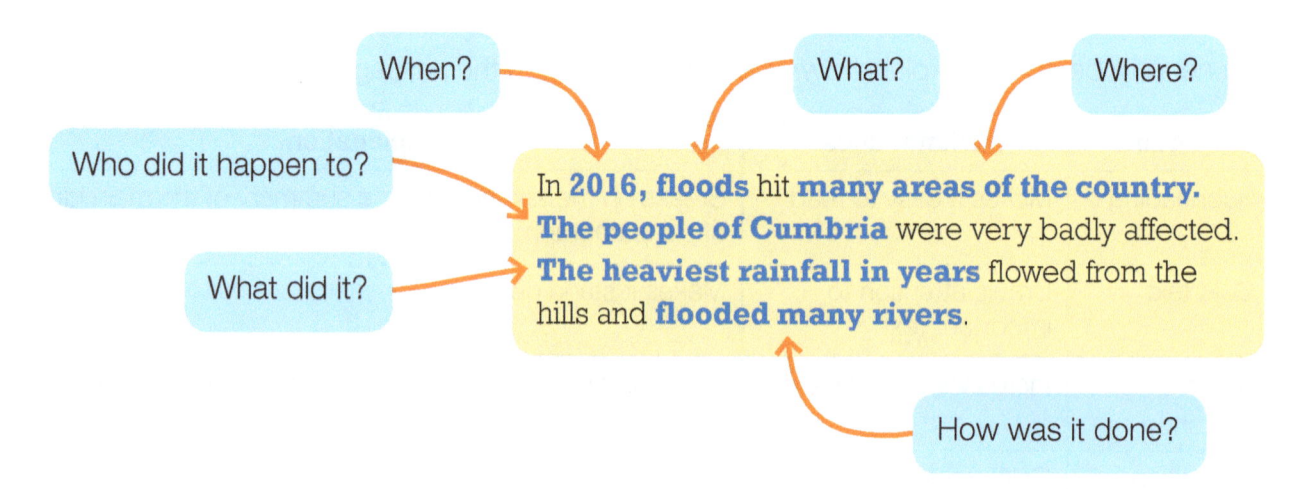

When? — What? — Where?
Who did it happen to?
What did it?

> In **2016, floods** hit **many areas of the country.** **The people of Cumbria** were very badly affected. **The heaviest rainfall in years** flowed from the hills and **flooded many rivers**.

How was it done?

In the next part of the story, the answers to the **motives** question are highlighted.

Why did it happen?

> **Rivers could not hold all of the rainfall** and **burst their banks**, overflowing into the towns.

The answers to the **facts** and **motives** questions can usually be found in the text. The **prediction** question is often not answered. You have to ask yourself that question. In this case, either something will be done to stop the rivers flooding or the same thing will continue to happen.

Activities

1. Write the answers to the following **facts** questions about this passage.

   > The Great Train Robbery took place in 1963. A gang of robbers stopped the mail train from Glasgow to London by changing the signal to red. In about twenty minutes they took 120 sacks from the train.

   a. When did the Great Train Robbery take place?
   b. What happened in the robbery?
   c. How many sacks did the robbers take off the train?

2. Write the answers to the following motives question in the next part of the passage.

   > The robbers escaped with over £2 million. This would be worth over £46 million today.

   Why did the gang want to rob the train?

3. Write down the answer to the following prediction question in this passage.

   > A huge man-hunt was organised and most of the gang were captured. Less than half a million pounds was ever found. The robbers were given long prison sentences in the hope that other people might be put off repeating their actions.

   What might other robbers do when they heard about the long sentences given to the gang members?

4. What are the possible answers to the prediction question in this passage?

   > When men first went to the Moon, it was to prove it could be done. Now there is talk of men returning there. This time it will be to learn about our past, and, possibly seeing our future.

   Give two things we might learn about if people ever go back to the Moon.

Reading 77

Planning writing

Learn

How do you plan writing?

To plan your writing start by:
- Deciding **what** you are writing about; **who** it is for; and what the best **form** of writing will it be aimed for. You will often be told all of this.
- Writing down ideas.
- Doing research if necessary.
- Organising your information.

Who are you writing for?: You wouldn't, for example, use the same language and style of writing for young children as you would for the prime minister. Look for the key words in the question to tell you who the audience is.

Key word – tells you **who** you are writing for.

> Write a letter to your **head teacher** asking for permission to hold a charity event in your school.

The best form of writing: This depends on what you are writing and who it is for. A sports report for a newspaper might be different to one for your school magazine. You have to decide if your writing is fiction or non-fiction. Then you need to think about its form and layout. Newspaper and magazine articles need columns. Letters look completely different. Advertisements often have pictures in them. Poetry can be almost anything! Again look for the key words in the question.

Key word: tells you **what** you are writing

> Write a **letter** to your head teacher asking for permission to hold a charity event in your school.

Writing down ideas: It doesn't matter how you do this, as long as you can understand it. Just make some notes of everything you can think of about your subject. You could make a list, draw a spider diagram; write some sentences or use sticky notes. Don't worry about the order; that can be sorted out later. These examples are all about the same subject.

Henry VIII
- Had 6 wives
- Father of Elizabeth I
- Made England a Protestant country

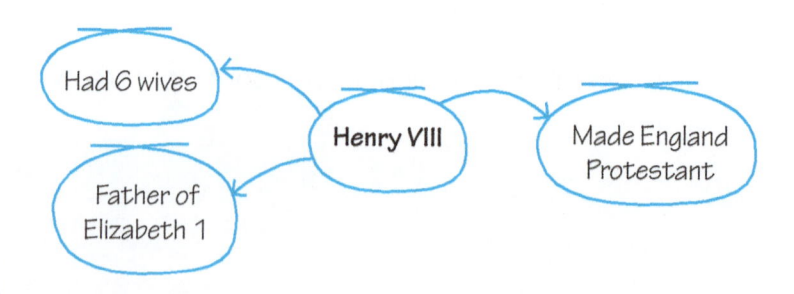

Had 6 wives — Henry VIII — Made England Protestant — Father of Elizabeth 1

Research and organisation: When you have written down what you already know, start to research further information to add to it. When you've finished, decide in which order you are going to use the information. You could make a bullet list to help you.

Activities

1. Decide who these pieces of writing are written for and explain how you know.

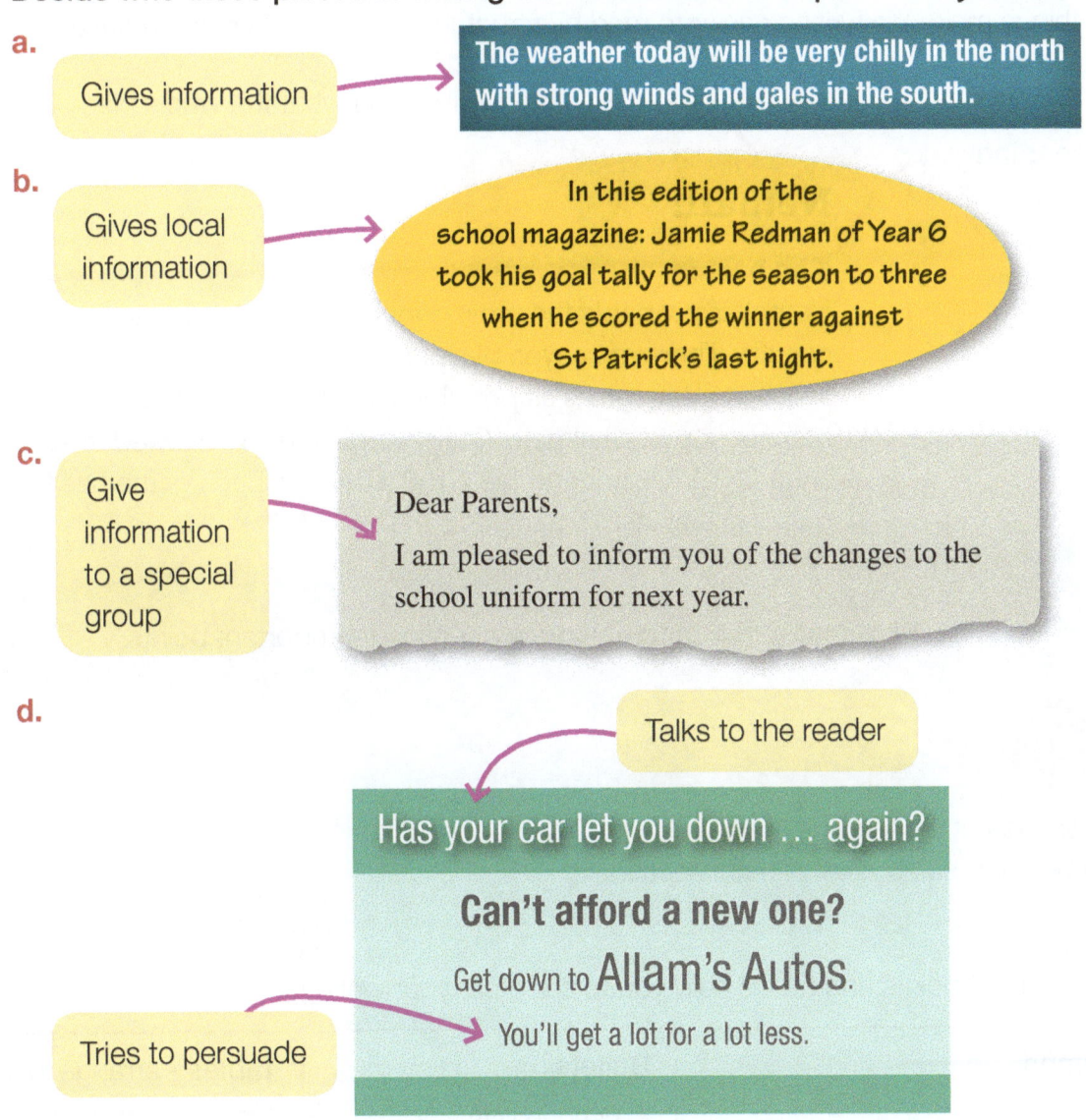

   a. Gives information → The weather today will be very chilly in the north with strong winds and gales in the south.

   b. Gives local information → In this edition of the school magazine: Jamie Redman of Year 6 took his goal tally for the season to three when he scored the winner against St Patrick's last night.

   c. Give information to a special group → Dear Parents, I am pleased to inform you of the changes to the school uniform for next year.

   d. Talks to the reader / Tries to persuade →

   Has your car let you down … again?

   Can't afford a new one?

   Get down to **Allam's Autos**.

   You'll get a lot for a lot less.

2. Make a spider diagram to plan for a subject of your own choice. Include at least five ideas and then write about them.

   Explain who your writing is for; which style of writing you have chosen; and how your piece fits that style.

> ✓ **Tip**
>
> Look for the key words in the question. They tell you what to write and how to write it.

Writing 79

Structuring writing

Learn

How do you structure writing?

To structure your writing use:
- structure – headings and subheadings
- presentation – highlighting, underlining, italics, bold text
- layout – boxes, columns, bullet points, or tables.

These things make the writing easier to read by structuring it. They often summarise the writing.

Heading – Tells you what the whole piece is about

Subheading – Gives a summary of this section

Netball!

The basics

Netball is probably the most popular game for girls in the country. There are seven players in each team. The aim is to score as many goals as possible by throwing the ball through a hoop on top of a tall pole. Only two players are allowed to score – the **Goal Attack** and the **Goal Shooter**. Each game has four quarters that last 15 minutes each.

italics, **bold text** and highlight – draw attention to important points

✓ Tip

The main idea of the text will be the heading. The subheadings should be short summaries of each section.

Columns, bullet points and tables help you to structure your writing.

Columns	**Bullets**	**Tables** - arrange ideas

Columns

Separate ideas and break up text, making it easier to read.

Can have headings. Can be different sizes.

Bullets
- used in lists
- make points clear
- help to summarise.

Tables - arrange ideas

Device	Use
Bullet point	Lists
Columns	Break up text
Tables	Lots of information

80 Writing

Activities

1. Give an appropriate heading for the whole passage and a subheading for the second paragraph.

   > Police in Lancashire are appealing for witnesses to an accident on the A59 near Preston yesterday. A lorry ran into a broken-down car, blocking the road for two hours.
   >
   > No one was injured but there was major damage to the central reservation and some street lights. Repairs to these are expected to take about two weeks to complete.

2. Rewrite this piece with a heading, two paragraphs and a subheading. Give reasons for your choices.

   > Diving at the Great Barrier Reef in Australia was one of the most exciting things I have ever done. Hundreds of people put on special blue suits to protect themselves from jellyfish stings and took to the water. Beneath the waves was the most beautiful world of coral. I was treated to palaces and fortresses; caverns and caves. Swimming along next to me were the most wonderful fish of all shapes and sizes. I wonder if they thought I was as magical as I thought they were.

3. Research the life of Joan of Arc. Make a bullet-pointed list of five things you could write about her. Choose two of those ideas and write a paragraph on each. Give your writing a heading and two subheadings and explain why you have chosen them.

4. Look at the following table with a partner. Discuss each of its points and decide which you think are the three most important ones. Choose alternative headings for each. Explain your decision to the rest of the class.

Dinosaurs	
Name	Dinosaur means terrible lizard but this is confusing because dinosaurs are not lizards at all.
Lived	They first appeared over 200 million years ago and were the dominant creatures on Earth for over 130 million years. They lived on every continent.
Types	Most people think there were only a few types, but scientists have identified over 500 different ones.
Size	Some were only 50cm long but the biggest dinosaurs at over 18 metres tall and almost 40 metres in length, were the biggest animals ever.
Food	Some dinosaurs ate meat but many ate only plants.

Writing 81

Building cohesion

Learn

What is cohesion?

Cohesion is when your writing links together and flows well. Cohesion is built by using different ways of joining our sentences and paragraphs.

A mechanic needs a toolbox to mend cars. In the toolbox will be spanners, screwdrivers, hammers, saws and lots of other useful tools. The mechanic may only use some of the tools occasionally because they have special uses. Other tools will be used every day. The tools are used to make the car run smoothly.

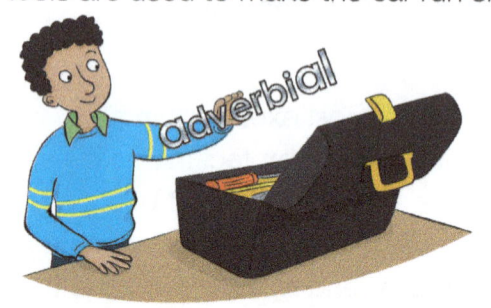

Now think of your writing. You have a toolbox as well. In it you have pronouns, adverbs, adverbials, conjunctions, synonyms, determiners and a whole lot more. Like the mechanic, you won't use all of them every day. You need to use your writing toolbox to choose the best tools to build cohesion and make your writing run smoothly.

Linking sentences
The easiest way to link sentences is by using conjunctions to join them together.

> The floods were really bad this year. The rain was heavy for weeks.

If we use a conjunction, the writing flows smoothly.

> The floods were really bad this year **because** the rain was heavy for weeks.

Conjunction – links the two sentences.

Linking paragraphs
A good way to link paragraphs is by using adverbials. These tell us straight away that the action has moved to another place or time.

> **In another part of the city**, the police searched a warehouse.

Adverbial of place tells us that the action has moved.

> **Some hours later**, the crooks were caught.

Adverbial of time tells us that time has moved on.

82 Writing

We can use adverbials to link ideas in non-fiction writing. For example, *on the other hand*, *in contrast*, or *as a consequence* all go back to previous ideas.

> In contrast, the results this year have been much better.

Repetition

Usually, repetition is not a good idea, but sometimes it can be used to create an effect.

> "The rule is: **jam tomorrow**, and **jam yesterday**, but never **jam today**"

Repetition links the ideas together

Lewis Carroll: *Alice through the Looking Glass*

Activities

Open your toolbox!

1. Rewrite this paragraph using pronouns to avoid repetition.

   > Tom met Katy at the school gate. Katy had done her homework but Tom hadn't. Katy and Tom decided that Tom had time to do it in the breakfast club.

2. Use conjunctions to link these sentences together into one long sentence.

   > I wanted to go to cinema.   I couldn't.   I didn't have enough money.

3. Use an adverbial of time to link these two ideas.

   > The teacher watched the class leave the room.   The next class arrived at the door.

4. Use an adverbial of place to link these two ideas.

   > Emily looked out of the window.   She could see the traffic passing by.

5. Write a short piece including all of these adverbials. You can use them in any order.

   > At the end of the street.   After school.   As quickly as I could.

6. Talk with a partner about how Sir Winston Churchill created an effect in this speech.

   > "This is not the end. It is not even the beginning of the end. But it is, perhaps, the end of the beginning."

Ellipsis

Learn

What is ellipsis?

Ellipsis is the omission of repeated, predictable or unnecessary words.

> Imagine this question has been asked: "Where are you going?"
>
> This reply could be: "I'm going to the skate park."
>
> Not every word of the reply is necessary. We could just say "To the skate park" or even "The skate park".

Sometimes words are repeated in a response.

> "Who was the prime minister in 1943?"
>
> You could answer:
>
> > "**The prime minister in 1943** was Winston Churchill" or just "Winston Churchill".
>
> These words are unnecessary because they just repeat the question.

In this sentence, **some** has been repeated when it doesn't need to be.

> We have bought **some** apples, **some** oranges, **some** bananas and **some** pears.
>
> The sentence could be:
>
> > We have bought some apples, oranges, bananas and pears.

Activities

1. **Copy these sentences. Then underline the unnecessary words.**
    a. My son was born at the start of this century, in 2001.
    b. I went because I wanted to go.
    c. My sister likes salad but I don't like salad.

2. **Copy and complete the answers to these questions.**
    a. "Do you want to go to the park?"   "____ we don't."
    b. "Have you finished your homework?"   "____ I have."
    c. "Who does the cooking in your house?"   "My dad ____."

3. **Write a short piece with lots of unnecessary words. Swap your piece with a partner. Highlight all of the unnecessary words in your partner's piece. Rewrite your partner's piece, making changes to take out the unnecessary words.**

Getting verbs right

> How do you get verbs right?

Learn

- Use the correct tense.
- Make sure that the subject and the verb agree.

Tense consistency: Use only one tense in a sentence.

They **booked** into their accommodation and **went** into the restaurant.

— both verbs in past tense —

Standard English: A singular subject (or person doing the action) must have a singular form of the verb.

Ted **visits** his grandparents. → Ted **was visiting** his grandparents.

one person – use the **singular** form of verb

A plural subject (or things doing the action) must have a plural form of the verb.

The children **clean** their teeth. → The children **were cleaning** their teeth.

many people – use the **plural** form of verb

For collective nouns, **one unit of** people – use the **singular** form of the verb.

The team **is playing** this morning. → The team **was playing** this morning.

> Make the verb ending agree with the number of doers!

Activities

1. Rewrite this piece of speech in Standard English: "I seen a bird in the garden."

2. Rewrite this sentence using the correct form of the verb to complete it.

   | is accompany   have accompanied   has accompanied   has accompanies |

   Amy ____ Jack to the concert.

3. Change the modal verb in this sentence to make it less likely to happen.

   I will win the 100 metres race on Sports Day.

Writing 85

Précising longer pieces of writing

Learn

What is précising?

To précis something, you find the main points of a piece of writing.
You rewrite the points briefly, usually using about one third of the words.

Sometimes, writers give more information than is necessary. These extra details can stop you understanding the main points easily. In this advertisement for a house, there are 106 words. The extra details have been highlighted.

> Brighton's Estate Agency: Semi-detached, two-bedroom bungalow for sale: £184,500. Price reduced! **Was £192,950 Now £184,500.** Beautiful Location – **Semi-detached true bungalow. Brighton's Estate Agency is delighted to offer for sale this semi-detached bungalow** set in the most sought-after location of Wapham. **There are two double bedrooms, both with views over the countryside**; a very spacious lounge – **perfect for parties**; and a dining area – **great for Sunday lunch with the family**. At the back **of the property** there is a great sized garden, **which has landscaping, lawns and flower beds**. **To appreciate the size, setting and location of this fantastic home, viewing is essential.**

When you take out the unnecessary additional details you are left with:

- Brighton's Estate Agency are selling a semi-detached, two-bedroom bungalow at a reduced price: £184,500.
- Beautiful location in Wapham.
- Spacious lounge, dining area and garden.

Now you have the main points, you have to rewrite the piece in about one third of the words.

> Brighton's Estate Agency is selling a semi-detached two-bedroom bungalow in a beautiful part of Wapham for the reduced price of £184,500. It has a large lounge; a dining area and a garden.

Activities

1. **Précis this text to show the main points in about fifty words.**

   > The Tower of London was built years and years ago – almost 1000 years to be more precise. It's home to the crown jewels. There are a lots of them. At the last count there were over 20,000 jewels. That's a lot of jewels! The Tower of London has often been used as a prison. Lots of people have been executed there but you may be surprised to learn that the last one was as recently as 1942! There used to be a royal zoo in the Tower. It was there for over 600 years and contained lions, kangaroo, polar bears, elephants and ostriches. Now the only animals in the Tower are ravens. It is said if they ever leave, the kingdom will fall, so the guards ensure they stay!

Choosing the right vocabulary and grammar

> How do you choose the right vocabulary and grammar?

Learn

Look at what you have written to see if you can improve it.
Make choices to make meanings clearer.

In the piece below, something doesn't sound right.

> My Auntie Sally has a big cat called Tigger. She is very hairy and likes climbing trees.

Who is very hairy and likes climbing trees: Auntie Sally or Tigger? It's not easy to tell! **She** could be either of them.

You can use correct grammar to make this clearer.

> My Auntie Sally has a big cat called Tigger, **who** is very hairy and likes climbing trees.

Now you know it's the cat who is hairy and likes climbing trees.

Sometimes you need a precise word to explain exactly what you mean.

> My mum has painted my wall **a nice shade of blue**.

This doesn't tell you much about the blue. If you need to know exactly what the colour was like, you could rewrite the sentence.

> My mum has painted my wall **a pale shade of sky blue**.

You can use a thesaurus to help you find the right word.

Activities

1. Rewrite this sentence to make it clear who is late.

   > When Sahid meets Tom at the park, he is always late.

2. Rewrite this piece, adding more detail so that it is clear to the reader what the gravestone looks like.

   > The gravestone was tall. It was a kind of grey colour. It had been there over a hundred years. The writing was hard to read.

3. **Use a thesaurus to help you improve a piece of writing you have already done.**

Writing 87

Describing settings and atmosphere

Learn

What are settings and atmosphere?

- Settings are where something takes place.
- Atmosphere is what it is like in that place.

Settings

The setting is the place you are describing. You have to tell the reader what is there. However, if you are not careful, this might sound like a simple list.

> Emma opened the door and stepped inside. It closed behind her. She could see a large chair, a table and a cupboard.

This needs more detail. The highlighted sections bring the room to life.

> Emma opened the **solid oak** door and stepped inside. It closed **like a dungeon door** behind her. **To her right** she could see a large chair, **it's once bright fabric now faded by the sun**. A **pine** table **with the remains of an evening meal spilled across it** stood next to the chair. **Behind both of them** was a large cupboard, **its mirrored doors swinging open to reveal**...

Atmosphere

This is more difficult to describe. This is about what the place feels like. The highlighted sections help the reader understand what it was like to be there.

> Emma opened the solid oak door and stepped **nervously** inside. It closed with **a sickening clang**, like a dungeon door behind her. To her right she could see a large chair, it's once bright fabric now faded by the sun, **all the life drained from it**. A pine table with the remains of an evening meal spilled across it stood next to the chair, **looking like someone left in a hurry**. Behind both of them was a large cupboard, its mirrored doors swinging open to reveal **a sight that chilled her to the bone**!

This poem shows us what the setting and atmosphere are like by using metaphors.

> The river was a swirling snake, curling through the land,
> The sea was a comfort blanket, covering the sand,
> The moon was a welcome lantern, held by a giant hand,
> And the smugglers' boat came bobbing...
>
> From *The Smugglers* by Graham Fletcher in the style of Alfred Noyes

The metaphors tell us what the setting was like by comparing it to something else.

Really good writing uses adjectives, adverbs, similes and metaphors to make the reader feel as if they are actually in the setting.

Make a description table

Sometimes it helps to make a description table to give you ideas.

The market – setting	Adjectives	Adverbs
Stalls	bright colourful crowded	noisily
People	cheerful persuasive	loudly cheekily
Weather	sunny glorious	sweatily

The market – atmosphere	Description	similes/metaphors
Movement	rushed slow ponderous	like a human snake; the crowd was a seething mass of predators
Sounds	shrill booming	a voice like a high-pitched whistle
Smells	tempting	the hot-dog van was a magnet, dragging me to it

Using the descriptions from the table you can make:

> In **glorious** weather, I walked past the **colourful**, **crowded** market stalls which were run by **persuasive** people who **cheekily** offered me the best deal in town. I was carried along by the **slow** crowd **that moved like a human snake** past the hot-dog van which **was a tempting magnet**, dragging me to it.

Activities

1. Make your own description table for other parts of the market. Use a thesaurus to help you find new words. Continue the story. Then label your writing to show the descriptions you have used to help the reader see and feel it.

2. With a partner, write two similes and one metaphor that describe your school.

3. In pairs, rewrite this passage adding to the setting and atmosphere. Use the example on page 88 to help you.

> The door to the pyramid was open. Professor Jones walked in. She looked around her. At first, she could see little in the darkness. As her eyes became accustomed to it, she saw treasure chests full of gold and silver. In the corner lay a complete mummy.

Think about how punctuation could add to the description.

4. Share your writing with another pair. Discuss why you have chosen your descriptions.

5. In pairs, rewrite your descriptions and read them to the rest of the class.

Describing characters and using dialogue

Learn

What are characters and dialogue?

- Characters are the people you write about.
- Dialogue is what they say.

Characters

It is very easy to describe a character using a list of physical features.

> The General was **a small man with short, dark hair.**

shows what he looks like

You get a picture of the character from this but if your characters are to become real people, you need to give much more information about how they move, their voices, feelings and emotions.

> He **limped with difficulty** towards the desk and **sat down wearily, with a sigh of relief**.

shows how he moves   shows how he feels

If you can throw in a bit of background to bring the character to life, even better!

> He stroked the scar on his cheek, a painful reminder of the last war.

✓ Tip

- Make a word picture. Have a picture in your mind of your character and paint it in words for your reader.
- Make a sound picture. Hear your character's voice in your head and tell your reader what it sounds like.

Dialogue

Your character needs to speak realistically but it's not just what characters say, it's how they say it that helps the reader build up a picture of them. Your readers need to be able to hear your character's voice. Most of us don't speak in Standard English, so it's likely that your character won't either.

> The General picked up the silver telephone that lay lifelessly on the desk. A few short stabs of his index finger dialled the number and he waited for the connection to be made. He closed his eyes in pain as the voice at the other end replied. This was his last chance to back out.
>
> "Do it," he said hoarsely. "Do it tonight."

Really good writing uses adjectives, adverbs, similes and metaphors to make the reader feel as if they are actually with the character.

The General seems to be a tired old man. If you make a description table, you can change him completely.

The character		
Features	hair scar eyes	thick, curly, wavy, oily purple, glowing, proud squinted, relief
Movement	legs finger	ran, raced, leaped, rapidly, contentment touches, strokes

The voice	
Sound	whispered, shouted, aggressively, decisively
Speed	quickly, slowly, ponderously, thoughtfully

This is the same text with some changes to the description.

> The General was a small man with **thick**, **oily** hair. He **ran rapidly** towards the desk and sat down quickly, with a sigh of **contentment**. He stroked the **glowing** scar on his cheek, a **proud** reminder of the last war.
>
> The General picked up the silver telephone that lay lifelessly on the desk. A few short **strokes** of his index finger dialled the number and he waited for the connection to be made. He **squinted** his eyes in relief as the voice at the other end replied. This was his last chance to back out.
>
> "Do it," he **whispered aggressively**. "Do it tonight!"

This General seems much younger and more aggressive. What does the exclamation mark at the end add to his character?

Activities

1. Make a description table for a spy who is searching an office for secret papers. Include descriptions of the spy's features, movements, emotions and voice.

2. Write a paragraph describing the spy searching the office.

3. Make a new description table for the spy. This time try to make them a completely different character.

4. Rewrite your paragraph using your new description table to change the descriptions.

5. Read your two paragraphs to a partner. Discuss what further changes you could make to improve them. Remember to think about similes, metaphors and punctuation. Choose one of your paragraphs and rewrite it with your partner to include all of the changes you have discussed.

Writing

Editing text

Learn

What is editing text?

Editing text is when you make changes to vocabulary, grammar and punctuation in order to improve the writing or to make the meaning clearer. When you write, you don't always get it right first time. Sometimes you make mistakes, you don't have enough detail or you just don't make the meaning clear. When you edit, you are looking for how to improve your writing.

There are lots of pieces in this text that need editing. They have been highlighted.

> A man with **a walking stick called Ted, was stood** at the end of the street. He pointed across the road at **a sign – red – with pictures on it – of children. It was a road sign – a warning sign**. He wished **he was** somewhere else because this was a school. **(He didn't like schools). He** saw another man. **He** was tall. **He were** carrying a newspaper. Ted ignored him. He pulled a list out of his pocket and **red** it.

Why do they need editing?

> A man with **a walking stick called Ted**

Not clear: Is it the man or the stick that is called Ted?

> **was stood** at the end of the street.

Tense error: There are choices here – Ted stood or Ted was standing.

> He pointed across the road at **a sign – red – with pictures on it – of children. It was a road sign – a warning sign**.

Overuse of dashes: makes the writing hard to read. It would be better as – He pointed at a red warning sign, with pictures of children on it, across the road.

> He wished **he was** somewhere else because this was a school.

This could be a tense error: The simple past tense, 'he was', is fine if it is an informal piece of writing. In a formal piece it should be the subjunctive form: 'he were'.

> **(He didn't like schools).**

Punctuation: Unnecessary use of brackets.

> **He** saw another man. **He** was tall. **He** was wearing carrying a newspaper.

Not clear: Who is the He?

> Ted ignored him. He pulled a list out of his pocket and **red** it.

Spelling mistake: should be read.

92 Writing

Activities

1. The highlighted parts of this story must be edited. Use the table of alternatives to edit it so that it has no mistakes and is clear. Give the piece a heading.

   > **In our house there are six of us. My parents, my gran, my sisters and me.** We have lived here for a long time. It was originally **my grandparents house** and **they were living here for a long time – at least sixty years I think but my dad says it could be a lot longer – nobody really knows.**

Original	Alternatives
In our house there are six of us. My parents, my gran, my sisters and me. Punctuation error.	Insert a colon followed by a list separated by commas or a colon followed by a bullet pointed list.
my grandparents house Punctuation error.	Insert an apostrophe of possession.
they were living here for a long time – at least sixty years I think but my dad says it could be a lot longer – nobody really knows. Not clear.	Précis this to summarise it and avoid repetition.

2. In this piece, the parts to be edited have been numbered. Make a table (like in question 1) to show the text to be changed; type of mistake; and your suggested alternatives.

   > Cuba is a magical island. It lie in the Caribbean Sea (1), not far from Florida; or the rest of America or Europe but a long way from Alaska (2). People who live three (3) are called Cubans. It is much bigger than people who have never been there think that it is (4). The main cities are Havana Varadero Santiago de Cuba and Santa Clara (5).

3. Swap a piece of your own writing with a partner. Edit and rewrite their work.

✓ Tip

Read the piece aloud to see what sounds odd. Don't think that your first piece is your finished piece. Think of it as a work in progress.

Proofreading

Learn

What is proofreading?

Proofreading is checking your writing to make sure there are no mistakes in it.

There are five main types of mistake:
- errors of spelling
- errors in the use of verb tenses
- errors in the use of punctuation
- errors in the use of grammar
- errors in the use of Standard English.

This text has lots of mistakes in it. They have all been highlighted.

weak: spelling error

was went: verb tense error

Last **weak** I **was went** to the **doctors**. **I seen** the doctor because I wasn't feeling **the best**.

doctors: punctuation error

the best: non-Standard English

I seen: grammar (subject/verb agreement)

It should have read:

Last **week** I **went** to the **doctor's**. **I saw** the doctor because I wasn't feeling **well**.

In addition, there are **ofeten thyping** or **ritting erros**. These happen when you know what you want to say but your fingers don't! By proofreading, you can spot the errors and put them right.

✓ Tip

Don't rely on a spellchecker. It won't pick up words that are spelled correctly but have the wrong meaning, like **weak** and **week** above.

Activities

1. This text contains lots of spelling mistakes and typing errors. Use a computer to retype it and then use a spellchecker to make the corrections. Which mistakes does the spellchecker not find?

   My farther once told me that I wood never fnid my fourtune with out a lot of had work. I spent the rest of my life trying toprove him wrong. I didn't mannage it. I eventuall had to admit that he was write.

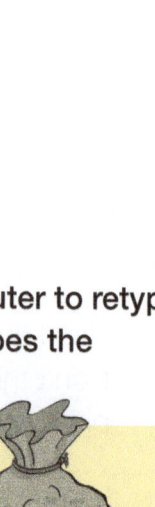

2. **This text contains a lot of verb errors. Rewrite it correctly.**

   I am sat at my desk. I often thinks it's a great place for looks out of the window. Across the road is where my friend, Carl, lives. I seen him last night. I've known him since I been small. I call him on the phone last night but he's not answering.

3. **This text has lots of punctuation mistakes. Rewrite it with the correct punctuation.**

   How do I explain newtons law of motion. There are lots of ways tell you show you do a demonstration. Whichever way i choose i know youll shout wow when I do?

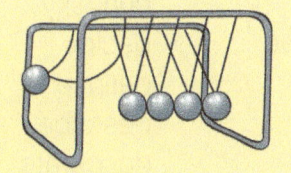

4. **This text has lots of different types of grammatical mistake. Rewrite it correctly.**

   We meet before we went to the match. We runs quick to make sure catches the buses. The match was an boring game. After the game we have waited for the bus. The bus is slow. We got home very later.

5. **This text has lots of mistakes in the use of Standard English. Rewrite it in formal language.**

   I ain't no fan of travelling. I dunno why folks rabbit on about it. There's an old geyzer near ours that reckons he's been every which where. It does me nut. IMHO home is best.

6. **This text has lots of different mistakes. Rewrite it without any of them.**

   I ain't got no hang-ups about school. Why do sum people wurry about it. You goes. You gets good results and you ends up with a good job. Where's the prob. I like like school. When I'm sat in lessons I'm really happy.

Writing 95

Word list

accident	conscience	foreign	muscle	regular
accidentally	conscious	forty	natural	reign
accommodate	consider	forward/	naughty	relevant
accompany	continue	forwards	necessary	remember
according	controversy	frequently	neighbour	restaurant
achieve	convenience	fruit	notice	rhyme
actual	correspond	government	nuisance	rhythm
actually	criticise	grammar	occasion	sacrifice
address	curiosity	group	occasionally	secretary
aggressive	decide	guarantee	occupy	sentence
amateur	definite	guard	occur	separate
ancient	describe	guide	often	shoulder
answer	desperate	harass	opportunity	signature
apparent	determined	heard	opposite	sincere
appear	develop	heart	ordinary	sincerely
appreciate	dictionary	height	parliament	soldier
arrive	different	hindrance	particular	special
attached	difficult	history	peculiar	stomach
available	disappear	identity	perhaps	straight
average	disastrous	imagine	persuade	strange
awkward	early	immediate	physical	strength
bargain	earth	immediately	popular	sufficient
believe	eight/eighth	important	position	suggest
bicycle	embarrass	increase	possess	suppose
breath	enough	individual	possession	surprise
breathe	environment	interest	possible	symbol
bruise	equip	interfere	potatoes	system
build	equipment	interrupt	prejudice	temperature
busy/business	equipped	island	pressure	therefore
calendar	especially	knowledge	privilege	thorough
category	exaggerate	language	probably	though/
caught	excellent	learn	profession	although
cemetery	exercise	leisure	programme	thought
centre	existence	length	promise	through
century	experience	library	pronunciation	twelfth
certain	experiment	lightning	purpose	variety
circle	explanation	marvellous	quarter	various
committee	extreme	material	question	vegetable
communicate	familiar	medicine	queue	vehicle
community	famous	mention	recent	weight
competition	favourite	minute	recognise	woman/women
complete	February	mischievous	recommend	yacht